# Goebel®

# Salt & Pepper Shakers

## Hubert and Clara McHugh

Schiffer Publishing Ltd

4880 Lower Valley Road, Atglen, PA 19310 USA

# Dedication

Dedicated to the youth of the world, as they represent the future of collecting.

The pricing in this book should be used only as a guide. Prices vary from one geographical location to another. The values shown attempt to reflect a normal range for each shaker. Neither the authors nor the publisher assumes responsibility for any losses incurred by the buyer or seller due to referring to this guide.

Hummel®, Goebel®, M.I. Hummel®, Goebel Collectors Club®, Insights Magazine©, Goebel figurines©, all trademarks found on page 7, and the Hummel Collectors Club® are registered trademarks of or copyrighted by W. Goebel Porzellanfabrik®, Germany. Their use herein is for identification purposes only. W. Goebel Porzellanfabrik® did not authorize this book nor furnish or approve of any of the information contained herein. The objects pictured in this book are from the collection of the authors of the book or various private collectors. This book is derived from the authors' independent research.

Published by Schiffer Publishing Ltd.
4880 Lower Valley Road
Atglen, PA 19310
Phone: (610) 593-1777; Fax: (610) 593-2002
E-mail: Info@schifferbooks.com

For the largest selection of fine reference books on this and related subjects, please visit our web site at
**www.schifferbooks.com**
We are always looking for people to write books on new and related subjects. If you have an idea for a book please contact us at the above address.

This book may be purchased from the publisher.
Include $3.95 for shipping.
Please try your bookstore first.
You may write for a free catalog.

In Europe, Schiffer books are distributed by
Bushwood Books
6 Marksbury Ave.
Kew Gardens
Surrey TW9 4JF England
Phone: 44 (0) 20 8392-8585; Fax: 44 (0) 20 8392-9876
E-mail: info@bushwoodbooks.co.uk
Free postage in the U.K., Europe; air mail at cost.

# Contents

# Acknowledgments

We wish to thank each and every person who contributed in any way toward the making of this book. Those contributors to the compilation of this pricing and identification guide are listed in alphabetical order below.

Gaye Adsett
Bill & Frances Clements
Toni Crittenden
Barbara Cummings
Nigel Dalley
Ann & Vern Ebner
John Ferry
Bill & Joyce Fisher
Goebel Collectors Club
Charlene Green
Helene Guarnaccia
Frances Hawkes
M. I. Hummel Collectors Club
Bob & Gail Jones
Ralph & Mildred Lechner
Mark & Georgeina Loderhose
Norma Montaigne
Elaine Moore
George & Dorothy Nemeth
Mike & Cathy Northcraft
Ron & Linda Rodolff
Fred & JoAnne Rose

Kay Smith
Gene & Marcia Smith
Ella Smothers & Bob T.
Diane Stary
Joe & Marie Strunk
Matthew Szynkiewicz
Frances Tawater
Irene Thornburg
Sylvia Tompkins

Thanks to all our children and Mom McHugh for putting up with a lengthy and detailed story about every "new" Goebel shaker that we found. Special recognition to our daughter Marie and husband Joe, who can spot a "Goebel®" across a crowded room in the pitch dark.

A special thank you to Nigel Dalley and Sylvia Tompkins for their extraordinary efforts to ship and bring their Goebel shakers to our house for photographing.

Last, but by no means least, we thank Goebel Porzellanfabrik® of Rodental, Germany, for the help we received through the following. The "Goebel Collectors Club" and Museum, which was located in Tarrytown, New York from the start of our research until its closing in 1989. To the "M.I. Hummel Club" personnel of Pennington, New Jersey, and the Club Magazine *Insights*®, for all the technical data, sculptor information, and the issue dates of shakers.

# Preface

The purpose of this book is to introduce you to all the salt and pepper shakers that we have become aware of in eighteen years of research that were produced by Goebel Porzellanfabrik® of Germany. Goebel® is a ceramic and porcelain manufacturer. Among hundreds of other items, they produce figurines based on certain paintings by Sister Maria Innocentia Hummel. (M.I. Hummel® figurines) While both the M.I. Hummel figurines and Goebel salt and pepper shakers carry similar trademarks, do not confuse the two. There is not, and never has been, any M.I. Hummel figurine produced as a salt or pepper shaker.

Where a photograph of a set was not available, we have still included the information on the shakers or other items in that set, in order to provide as complete a listing as possible. If readers have additional information or photographs of those sets not shown, we would love to hear from them in order to potentially include this material in a second edition of the book.

We have attempted to place a range of value on all sets except those that are not shown. Pricing information was gathered through extensive travel and shopping, by frequenting antique and collectibles shows, by attending and participating in twenty salt and pepper collector's conventions, by searching flea markets and junk shops, and also by corresponding with collectors throughout the world.

The values as presented reflect primarily U.S. prices east of the Mississippi. Prices are higher in those sections of the country and the world where distribution of new pieces was sparse. Further, the distribution of Goebel salt and peppers has been sometimes "spotty," as evidenced by certain sets commonly found in New Zealand, for instance, that are not found in any other country, and condiment sets that are fairly plentiful in England but non-existent in the United States.

Readers who desire to meet other collectors of salt and pepper shakers should consider joining the Novelty Salt & Pepper Shakers Club, an international organization of 1300 members. The Club publishes a quarterly newsletter, holds an annual convention in different locations each year, and sponsors local chapters that provide opportunities for interacting more frequently with others who love this hobby. For more information, visit the Club's Web site at www.saltandpepperclub.com or contact the authors via e-mail (littlenbig@bigfoot.com).

# Glossary and Prefixes
## Pertaining to Salt & Pepper Shakers

**BULL** — Based on designs by artist LIZ BUL.

**BYJ** — Based on a painting by the Pennsylvania artist CHARLOTTE BYJ (pronounced BY)

**Dep** — Depose (French) means to deposit or leave a mark, therefore to register a trademark.

**DIS** — Based on a design by WALT DISNEY.

**DRGM** — "Deutsches Reichs Gebrauchs Modell," which translates approximately to "German Empire Utensil Model," i.e., kitchen utensil.

**E** — Egg Cups, or sets with Egg Cups and Salt & Pepper Shakers.

**GOEBEL**® — The ceramic manufacturer that makes Goebel® and M.I. Hummel® figurines.

**G** — Mustard Pots.

**GRA** — Based on designs by HILDA GRAY, a free lance sculptor.

**Hei** — Based on designs by HERMAN HEINDL.

**Hol** — Holzapfel (means crabapple), a nickname for Ruth Fetzer.

**Hummel**® — Figurines based on paintings by Sister Maria Innocentia Hummel (1909-1946). (NO Hummel® salt and pepper shakers were ever made.)

**KAU** — Based on designs by cartoonist ROLF KAUKA.

**L** — The "City" series. The second letter is always the first letter of the city.

**L Mun** — Munich Children series. Also L Muen and L Munch.

**MAR** — Hanilore Marek.

**M** — ON or IN something

**M/GRA** — GRA sets that are ON or IN something.

**Na** — NASHA, a series based on designs by artist ERNA REIBER.

**P** — Most of the salt and peppers pairs are preceded by "P"

**S** — Pitchers and Mustard Pots.

**T** — Trays, Cups, and Coffee Pots.

**Tri** — Based on designs of WALTER TRIER

**Well** — Based on designs of HANNS WELLING

**XP** — Place Card Holders.

**Z** — Sugar Bowls.

# Trademarks — Dating and Identification

The trademarks used on Goebel® salt and pepper shakers range from an incised Crown Mark first used in 1923 to the mark introduced in 1991. The marks can be used as an aid in dating your particular set. Those used on shakers have been broken down into eight categories numbered TM (Trademark) 1 to 8.*

TM 1 is the CROWN MARK. It may be incised (impressed) or just stamped on the bottom. 1923-1949.

TM 2 are the several varieties of FULL BEE MARKS, used between 1950-1959.

          (third variety)

1950-1954     1955-1956     1957-1958

1958     1959

TM 3 is a STYLIZED BEE in a V, in three varieties, used between 1960-1972.

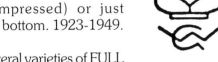

1960-1963     1960-1972

W. Germany

1960-1972

TM 4 is also called the THREE LINE trademark.

1964-1972

TM 5 includes the last use of the BEE.

1972-1978

TM 6 was brought out in 1979 and used up to 1991. This mark was often just a sticker and not stamped or impressed.

TM 7 brings back the CROWN as part of the mark.

1991-1999  

Paralleling "Occupied Japan" objects are those made in Occupied Germany between 1946 and 1948. These SPECIAL marks can date a set within two years.

TM 8 is the current trademark. 2000-  

*SOURCE: Insights Magazine©

# Identification

The most obvious means of spotting and identifying a Goebel® S&P is to observe one of the BEE marks on the bottom. Refer to page 7 for the variety that may be found on salt and peppers. The trademarks and numbers are ALWAYS FOUND ON THE BOTTOM of the shaker. Occasionally the sculptor is marked on the back. The set cannot be older than the trademark on it, nor can it be older than the first release date. Another clue to age is that seven and five holes were used before World War II , three and two were used after the war.

Trademarks 2, 3, 4, and 5 will usually be stamped. Trademark 1 will most often be incised (impressed) into the object. Trademarks 6 and 7 may be in the form of a sticker, especially on the small shakers.

There **was** a mold number on each object as it was molded, however many numbers were partially or completely "washed off" when the newly molded object was cleaned up before being fired. LOOK FOR THIS NUMBER. Look in the light, but since bright light sometimes glares off the bottom, also look in the dark. Turn your back to the light, shade the object, roll it around, turn it, and to your amazement sometimes the numbers will suddenly appear.

The numbering system usually starts with one letter, has two or three numbers, and often ends with a /A or /B.

The number is NEVER ON THE BACK, the word Germany is NEVER INCISED, and a FOUR NUMBER system with no preceding letter is not Goebel®.

The number on a particular object can vary, depending on whether it was issued as a part of a condiment set (with the prefix "M") or as an S & P (with the prefix "P").

About 1973, Goebel developed a new numbering system. They replaced the prefix "M" with the number 77 for four piece sets and 78 for three piece sets, and they replaced the prefix "P" with the number 73; i.e., the newest version of P 189 became 73 189.

CORKS: Corks can be misleading, as anyone could have put the wrong stopper in a shaker. However, if the quality seems to be there but no mold number or BEE stamp can be found, the stopper may be the missing clue. Goebel has used a unique stopper since the early 1950s that is plastic and is "coined" around the outer edge. There are a few slightly different size stoppers.

A correct PAIR is NEVER IDENTICAL. At least the hole pattern will be different. If the objects are different, as in set P 155, the numbers will be the same and the "slash A" and "slash B" will prove them to be a set.

COLORS: Goebel used six basic colors for many years and you will learn to spot them as you hunt the elusive S & P's. White, black, yellow, blue, green, and orange were used on older sets. The browns, reds and in between shades are more recent developments.

# Pricing

The prices listed in this book are based on the values of PERFECT SETS. Unless a piece is rare, a damaged piece has very little value. Our estimate of a "pair" with one damaged piece is 1/2 price. (Pay for the good pieces only.)

Singles (Half Pairs): If you do not have the mate, pay considerably less that 1/2. If you DO have the other piece, then pay slightly more than 1/2 to complete the pair.

Singles, issued as single pieces; These must be judged as complete pieces and are priced as such.

Incomplete Sets: If you find a good pair on a chipped tray or broken basket, try to determine if it was issued as a pair only, and then use the value of the pair.

This is a "Value Guide," based on our experience and observation of prices actually paid. Each set is worth that price agreed to by a WILLING BUYER and a WILLING SELLER.

# The Salt & Pepper Shakers

## Alphabetical Order

BYJ 31 — "The Sleigh Ride," Gingerbread Boy and Girl on a Sled, by Ewald Wolf in 1957. Based on artist Charlotte Byj's work. Rare. $3,000.00 to $4,000.00

Bull 323 — Katzenjammer Kids and the Captain Condiment Set, contrived by Ewald Wolf in 1969, based on the artwork of Liz Bul. Rare. $3,000.00 plus or minus.

BYJ 30 — Girl with a Muff, by Ewald Wolf in 1958. Based on a painting by Charlotte Byj. Rare. $3,000.00 to $5,000.00.

BYJ 32 — Snow Man and Snow Woman, sculpted by Ewald Wolf in 1958, from Charlotte Byj's artwork. Rare. $1,200.00 to $1,700.00

DIS 32 (sitting) & DIS 34 — Thumper with Eyes Closed, based on Walt Disney characters. Reinhold Unger shaped these in 1950. $125.00

DIS 33 A & B — Flower the Skunk. Reinhold Unger sculpted the set from Walt Disney characters in 1950. $95.00

DIS 40 —Thumper with Eyes Open, based on Walt Disney characters and shaped by Reinhold Unger in 1950. $100.00

DIS 41 (erect) & DIS 50 — Thumper reared back on his haunches, based on Disney characters. It was 1950 when Reinhold Unger created these and several other Disney characters in three dimensions. $150.00

DIS 138 A & B — Figaro on his Basket. Reinhold Unger wove the basket in 1950. $125.00

DIS 204 A B C —Thumper in the new style small Oval Basket, red Salt and yellow Pepper. The same mold as for DIS 40 was used for this three piece set. $45.00

E 107 A Chick Salt on E 107 B Egg Cup. $40.00 to $50.00

DIS 180 A & B — Davy Crockett and a Bear with tongue protruding. It was 1950 when Arthur Moeller put the rifle in Davy's hands. Extremely rare. $1,200.00 to $2,000.00

E 108 A Rabbit Salt, and E 108 B is the E 107 B Egg Cup. The "cups" were also available in a set of six cups. $50.00 to $60.00

E 120 — Egg Cup Set with shaker and spoon. $25.00 to $35.00

*Above and below:*
E 124 — Egg Cup Set consists of two cups, one P 500 small Bird by Karl Simon in 1926, and one P 490 little Duck by Erich Wohner in 1925. Unique. $75.00 to $100.00

E 151 A B C — Egg Cup Set, with a Tiny Cat as Salt and Tiny Dog as Pepper. Scarce. $95.00+

GRA 109 B & C — Salt & Pepper Shakers are based on Hilda Gray's artwork. $10.00

E 231 A B C — Egg Cup Set has the Chick as Salt Shaker, a loose egg cup, and a tray with spoon. $20.00 to $25.00

GRA 123 A & B — Dressed Fox was sculpted by Wolfgang Ebert in 1963. The prefix indicates "Hilda GRAy." $75.00 to $85.00

GRA 124 A & B — Squirrels, shaped by Wolfgang Ebert in 1963. Scarce.

---

GRA 125 A & B — Spiffy Rabbits were also created by Wolfgang Ebert in 1963, based on Miss Gray's work. $75.00

GRA 128 A & B — "German" Boy and Girl, based on artwork by Hilda Gray and formed in 1964 by Wolfgang Ebert. $75.00

GRA 127 A & B — Chef and Cook, created in 1964 by Wolfgang Ebert. $100.00

GRA 129 A & B — Scandinavian Boy and Girl, by Wolfgang Ebert in 1964, based on Hilda Gray's work. $75.00

GRA 147 A & B — "Tower" Salt & Pepper Shakers, by Wolfgang Ebert and Hilda Gray in 1966. $35.00

GRA 174 — Condiment Set.

GRA 178 A & B — Tall Cylinders.

GRA 179 A & B — Short Cylinders, by Wolfgang Ebert and Hilda Gray, in 1966. $22.00

GRA 189 A & B — Erect Ducklings, by Hilda Gray and shaped by Wolfgang Ebert in 1964. $45.00

GRA 195 A & B — Large and Small Roosters, hatched in 1967 by Wolfgang Ebert. $65.00

GRA 197 A & B — Stylized Chicks.

HEI 10 is HEI 1 A B C on the T 69 long Oval Tray.

HEI 11 — Standing Chimps, sculpted by Oskar Hoernlein in 1962.

GRA 204 A & B — Tapered Shakers, by Wolfgang Ebert in 1968, based on artwork of Hilda Gray. $18.00

HOL 19 A B C — Small Fish on Tray T 71/1. The HOL prefix stands for "Holzapfel" which is the "nickname" or "pet name" for Ruth Fetzer. Treutner sculpted the pair in 1956. $22.00

HEI 1 A B C D — Happy Chimp Condiment Set. Oskar Hoernlein was the sculptor who shaped the "Monkeys," based on the artwork of Herman Heindl.

HEI 1 B & C — Happy Sitting Chimp Shakers are part of the Condiment Set. $20.00 to $30.00

HOL 73 A B C D — Odd shaped Condiment Set. The "handles" are lumps shaped on the side of each piece. Horst Aschermann created the set in 1955, from Ruth Fetzer's work. $75.00

HOL 78 A B C D — Water Buckets and Watering Can on a Clover Shaped Tray. Ruth Fetzer was the artist who inspired sculptor Oskar Hoernlein. $65.00 to $85.00

HOL 79 A B C D — Fish, Buoy, and Bait Bucket on a Boat Shaped Tray. Holzapfel was the inspiration for the set, by Treuntner. $100.00+

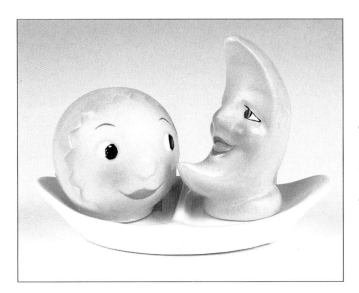

HOL 87 A & B — Striped Half Eggs.

HOL 80 A B C — Sun and Moon on Tray T 71/0, by Naumann and Treuntner in 1958. $65.00

18

HOL 88 A & B — Clown Faces, made up by
Helmut Wehlte in 1959. Scarce. $125.00

LE 16 A & B — Boy and Girl dressed as in the Alsace region of
France, by Reinhold Unger in 1950. $40.00.

KAU 11 — Stylized Seal
Condiment Set, based
on cartoonist Rolf
Kauka's comic strips.
Karl Wagner whipped
up the set in 1958.
$160.00

KAU 33 A & B — Boy and Girl are
based on Kauka's work. $125.00

LE 268 A & B — The "L" designates that this is from
the "Land" series. The next letter is the first letter of the
region that the set represents. Can you guess what part
of France the set represents? $100.00+

19

L Mun 22 A & B — Munich (Young Boy) Monks, by Reinhold Unger in 1938. $40.00

L Mun 27 A & B — Steins with Flowers, shaped by Reinhold Unger in 1938. $18.00

L Mun 28 A & B — Steins with Hearts, created by Reinhold Unger in 1938. $18.00

L Mun 31 A B C D — Munich Condiment Set on a Triangle Tray, by Reinhold Unger in 1938. Note that the rutabaga is in the right hand. $125.00.

L Mun 45 A B C D — Munich Condiment Set on a Clover Shaped Tray, by Reinhold Unger in 1938. The rutabaga is in the left hand. $125.00

LN 112 — Kookaburra Bird. Rare. $100.00 (single example found)

L Mun 124 — Large Munich Monk Shaker. Rare. $200.00+

LN 114 — Kangaroos. LN = Land New Zealand and Australia. Rare. $100.00 each

M 1 — Spherical Condiment Set, comes in at least three colors: orange, light blue and (as seen here) black. Reinhold Unger created the set in 1934. $50.00 to $150.00

M 6 A B C D — Holland Condiment Set, consists of an octagonal "Windmill" Mustard Pot and a Dutch Boy and Girl Salt & Pepper by Arthur Moeller, on Max Pechtold's 1927 Tray. $500.00+

M 8 A B C D — Sailboat Condiment Set, by Erich Lautensack in 1936.

M 2 A B C D — Mushroom Condiment Set on a Clover Shaped Tray. The shakers are P 420/0 & P 420/2/0 by Reinhold Unger in 1927. Karl Simon designed the Mustard Pot in 1934. The set was created by placing the pieces on the tray that Max Pechtold formed in 1927. A ceramic spoon was added, and the value is $95.00.

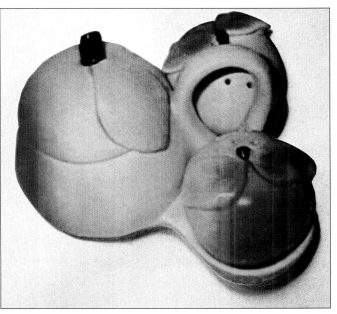

M 9 A B C — Apple Condiment Set. Erich Lautensack planted these in 1936. Scarce. $50.00 to $60.00

M 3 A B C — Mustard Pot and Salt & Pepper, similar to M 1. Whipped up by Arthur Moeller in 1934.

M 10 A B C — Pear Condiment Set, grown by E. Lautensack in 1936.

M 4 A B C — Comprised of an Airship Tray with People Salt & Pepper Shakers. Flown by A. Moeller in 1934.

M 11 A B C D — Mushroom Condiment Set, consists of M 2 A B C in a deep tray with a central tall handle.

M 12 A B C — Tomato Condiment Set with a ceramic spoon. Erich Lautensack is credited with shaping the set in 1937. $80.00

---

M 13 — Has S 19/0 as the Condiment Pot.

---

M 14 A B C — Ceramic imitation wicker should have a cover and a ceramic spoon. Rare. $50.00

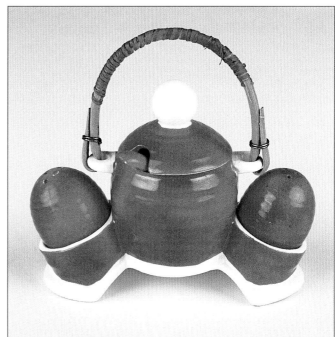

M 15 A B C — With cover and ceramic spoon. Similar to M 14, but with real wicker handle. Rare. $50.00

---

M 16 A B C D — Bee Hive Condiment Set.

---

M 17 A B C D — Consists of P 37 A & B Salt & Pepper on a tray with a "Dutch" Mustard Pot.

---

M 18 A B C — Pig Condiment Set. The ceramic spoon is the pig's curly tail.

---

M 19 — Man's Face Condiment Set.

---

M 20 A B C D — Reinhold Unger came up with this set and Triangle Shaped Tray in 1938. $65.00

M 21 A B C D — Dog Salt Shaker, Barrel Pepper Shaker, Boat Shaped Tray, and Barrel Mustard Pot with Spoon, by Reinhold Unger in 1938. Rare. $200.00+

M 22 A B C D — Munich Condiment Set, with L Mun 27 Salt and L Mun 28 Pepper Shakers, on M 20 D Tray. $40.00

M 23 A B C — Fish Condiment Set with the spoon as its fin, by Arthur Moeller in 1939. $45.00

M 24 A B C D — Pots of Flowers Condiment Set, developed by Arthur Moeller in 1946. Rare. $150.00+

M 25 A B C — Consists of Arthur Moeller's P 108 A & B placed on Tray T 71/1 in 1950. $25.00

M 26 A B C — This is the 1950 grouping of P 95 A & B on Tray T 71/1. $60.00

M 27 A B C — Assembled by placing P 91 A & B on the T 71/1 Tray. $35.00

M 28 A B C — Golfer on a "Golf Club" Tray was originally produced with a tan ball Pepper Shaker and a grey pants golfer Salt Shaker. $85.00 to $100.00

M 28 A B C — Later editions of Karl Wagner's 1957 set had a golfer with blue pants and a white ball. $85.00 to $100.00

M 31 A B C — Chef Holding Pots was cooked up by Hans Zetzmann in 1953. $65.00 to $90.00

M 29 — Condiment Set.

M 30 A B C — Cable Car Condiment Set with a "Tower" Tray was sculpted in 1953 by Arthur Moeller. $60.00 to $80.00

M 32 A B C — Bellboy with two Suitcases was issued with "Excelsior" on his hat. $225.00 to $250.00

M 33 A B C — Chinaman holding two "Lantern" Shakers. The 1952 set was designed by Hans Zetzmann. $75.00

M 35 A B C — Same as M 32 except for the name on his cap. This one reads Sheraton. $225.00 to $250.00

M 34 A B C — Pineapples on Pineapple Plant Tray, also designed by Hans Zetzmann in 1953. $45.00+

M 36 A B C — Squirrel Salt and Pine Cone Pepper, on a Leaf Tray, by Karl Wagner in 1953. $50.00

M 37 — One Piece Toilet with Wooden Lid Mustard, and "P" Pot open Salts, created in 1953. No sculptor admits making this unusual set. Rare. $100.00+

M 38 A B C D — Pepper Shaker, Open Salt, and Mustard Pot on a Round Tray, by Theo Menzenbach in 1954. $75.00 to $100.00

M 40 — Tulip Mustard and Tulip Salt & Pepper Condiment Set.

M 41 — Consists of M 40 Tray with P 98 Salt & Pepper Shakers. The Tulip Mustard was grown by Schumann in 1953 and nurtured by Reinhold Unger's three-year-old Watering Cans. Rare. $150.00+

M 42 A B C D — First issued in 1954 with Friars that wore sandals exposing their toes, designed by Reinhold Unger. This early version has the RARE Ceramic Spoon. $75.00 to $125.00 w/toes AND SPOON.

M 42 A B C D — Set was soon redesigned in 1955 to eliminate the toes, and the extra painting required. The Mustard Pot still split at the shoulders. $55.00

M 42 A B C D — Produced as Cardinal Tuck from 1960-1965. These are much scarcer than the Friars, and are worth more. $200.00 to $350.00

M 44 A B C — Consists of LE 268 Salt & Pepper on a Stork Tray. Scarce. $125.00+

M 46 A B C D — Elephant Condiment Set by Oskar Hoernlein in 1955, on M 355 Tray. $150.00

29

M 47 A B C — Apple Condiment Set, by Ewald Wolf in 1965, is quite reminiscent of M 9. $50.00

M 48 A B C D — Santa Condiment Set was a gift of Oskar Hoernlein in 1965. The tray is identical to T 69. Scarce. $175.00 to $200.00

M 49 A B C — Consists of P 154 A & B on Tray T 71/1. $22.00

M 50 A B C — Consists of P 130 A & B on Tray T 71/1. $50.00

M 51 A B C — Includes a tray to hold the pair of Dutch Clogs.
Karl Wagner was the shoemaker, in 1955. Scarce. $125.00

M 55 A B C D — Rabbit Condiment Set on M 42 D Tray. $80.00

M 52 A B C D — This is on the M 52 D Tray. 1956 was the year
Helmuth Wehlte monkeyed around with this set. $90.00

M 53 A B C — Created by placing M 47
B & C on the T 71/1 Tray. $45.00

M 56 A B C — Fisherman with Baskets of Fish. Karl Wagner and Naumann trolled for this Condiment Set in 1956. $95.00

M 57 A B C D — Dog and House Condiment Set was conceived by Oskar Hoernlein in 1956. $125.00

M 58 A B C D — Fox, Duck, and Tree Stump on the T 69 Tray. Oskar Hoernlein whipped this up in 1957. $125.00

M 59 A B C D — Fruit Condiment Set by Naumann, in 1956. The Tray, M 59 D is used on many other Goebel condiment sets. $85.00

M 60 A B C — An assembly of T 71/1 Tray, P 163 A Salt Shaker, and P 163 B Pepper Shaker. $75.00

M 61 A B C D — Acorn Condiment Set. The Shakers are "Stackers," and along with the Mustard Pot they sit on an Oak Leaf Tray. Treutner did these. $75.00 to $80.00

M 62 A B C D — Walrus Condiment Set was found in Australia. Rare. $500.00+

M 63 A B C — Tossed together in 1960 by placing M 55 B & C on the Oval T 71/1 Tray. $45.00

M 64 A B C D — Condiment Set based on the Dickens character "Pickwick." Arthur Moeller and Oskar Hoernlein got together and created this set in 1956. Scarce. $300.00 to $350.00

M 66 A B C — Hen and Chicks Condiment Set was hatched by Helmuth Wehlte in the late 1950s. $90.00 to $110.00

M 65 A B C — Sits on the Kidney Shaped Tray M 65 D. Arthur Moeller and Oskar Hoernlein collaborated to create this set in 1966. Scarce. $350.00 400.00

M 67 A B C — A Butcher selling Salty Ham and Peppery Sausage. Helmuth Wehlte cooked up the set in 1956. $95.00 to $120.00

M 68 A B C — Also put together in 1956 by Helmuth Wehlte. The Lady Mustard would love to sell you her Flowers. $100.00 to $125.00

M 69 A B C — Chef Condiment Set, created by Manfred Wittig in about 1959. $80.00

M 70 A B C — Tennis Player and Ball on a "Racquet" Tray, by Helmuth Wehlte in the late 1950s. $85.00 to $100.00

M 72 A B C D — Chianti Bottle Condiment Set, assembled by a group of sculptors in 1958. $40.00

M 73 A B C D — Harlequins with Black Collars on M 42 D Tray, by Master Sculptor Gerhard Skrobek in 1959. $75.00

M 76 A B C D — Cat and Kittens Condiment Set.

M 77 A B C D — Fisherman and Fish Condiment Set on Oyster Shell Tray, by Helmuth Wehlte in 1959. $150.00 to $175.00

M 78 A B C D — Cat and Mice Condiment Set on M 59 D Tray, by Arthur Moeller in 1959. $150.00+

M 79 A B C D — Boy, Dog, and Cat in Barrels, by Helmuth Wehlte in 1959. $225.00 to $250.00

M 83 A B C — Oranges on T 80 Tray.

M 84 A B C — Condiment Set.

M 86 A B C D — Condiment Set with Veggies on top. The 1960 Set is by Gerhard Skrobek. $60.00

M 86 — Variation is the same set, painted to give the impression of cherries. $60.00

M 89 A B C — "Sheaves of Wheat," by Oskar Hoernlein in 1960. $40.00

M 90 A B C D — Cat, Chick, and Rabbit Condiment Set was created by Naumann in 1960. $95.00

M 91 A B C D — Boy, Girl, and Beach Ball Condiment Set, by Naumann in 1960. Rare. $350.00 to $500.00

M 96 A B C D — Flower Pot Condiment Set, by Gerhard Skrobek in 1961. $85.00

---

M 92 — Black Face Condiment Set, by H. Eber in 1960.

---

M 100 A B C — Stylized Chickens with NO tray assigned, shaped by Arthur Moeller in 1946. $85.00

---

M 101 — Fish Condiment Set, by Oskar Hoernlein, in 1962.

---

M 104 A B C D — Pigs on T 69 Tray, by Karl Wagner in 1962.

---

M 93 A B C D — Wheat Condiment Set, attributed to a group in 1960. $65.00

M 106 — Cow Condiment Set, raised by Oskar Hoernlein in 1962. $70.00 to $90.00

M 111 A B C D — Rabbit Condiment on M 59 D Tray by Karl Wagner and Rothling in 1962. $75.00

M 107 A B C D — Duck Condiment Set on T 76 Tray, created in 1962 by Karl Wagner. $60.00

M 112 — Cake ? Or Chick ? Condiment Set by Oskar Hoernlein in 1963.

M 108 A B C D — Standing Pig Condiment Set, on M 59 D Clover Shaped Tray.

M 109 — Slim Oval Condiment Set, quite similar to M 114 except for the decorated pattern.

M 110 A B C — Consists of M 89 B & C on M 88 C Tray.

M 113 — Consists of M 111 B & C Rabbits on T 92 Tray, attributed to Karl Wagner and Rothling in 1963. $70.00

M 114 A B C D — Striped Condiment
Set on M 59 D Tray. $35.00 to $50.00

M 115 A B C D — Squirrel Condiment
Set, by K. Wagner in 1965 $75.00

M 116 — Pink Pigs, created by Gerhard Skrobek in 1965.

M 117 A B C — The Pink Pigs on T 71/1 Tray. $35.00

M 118 A B C D — Hedgehog Condiment Set, whipped up by
Wolfgang Ebert in 1967.

M 119 B C D — Consists of P 153/I Large & P 153/O Small Friar
on T 71/1 Tray. $25.00 to $30.00

M 119 B C D — Variation in blue. $35.00 to $40.00

M 120 — Consists of P 150 A & B on T 71/1 Tray. $26.00

M 202 A B C — Has M 90 B & C Rabbit and Chick in the small Oval Woven Basket. $22.00

M 201 A B C — Consists of M 89 B & C Sheaves of Wheat in the small Oval Woven Basket. $30.00

M 203 A B C — Consists of P 180 A Stylized Duck and P 180 B Stylized Fox in the small Oval Woven Basket. $135.00

M 204 A B C — Consists of 71 204 A & B Red and Yellow Rabbits in the small Oval Woven Basket. $60.00

M 206 A B C D — This is M 86 A B C Shakers With Vegetables on top in the long Oval Woven Basket. $75.00

M 209 A to E — Has five pieces in a basket.

M 210 A B C D — Includes M 93 A and M 89 B & C Sheaves of Wheat in the long Oval Woven Basket.

M 211 A to E — Has five pieces in a Square Woven Basket.

M 212 A B C — Made up of P 420 I & O Large and Small Mushrooms in the small Oval Woven Basket. $32.00

M 213 A B C — Has M 47 B Apple and M 59 C Pear in the small Oval Woven Basket $40.00

M 214 A B C — Consists of M 86 A & B Shakers With Vegetables on top in the small Oval Woven Basket. $35.00

M 216 A B C — Consists of P 150 A & B Carp in the large Oval Woven Basket. $23.00

M 215 A B C — Is P 179 A & B Sitting Cats in the small Oval Woven Basket. $30.00

M 217 A B C — Has P 184 A & B Cats in the small Oval Woven Basket. $28.00

M 218 A B C — Made up of P 190 A & B Eggs in the large Oval Woven Basket. $30.00

M 222 A B C D — Consists of M 100 A B C in the Long Woven Basket. $90.00 to $100.00

M 224 A B C D — Has the P 176 Friars carrying books and X 101 toothpick holder in the Long Woven Basket.

M 225 A B C D — Consists of P 420 I & O with X 33 toothpick holder in the Long Woven Basket.

M 219 A to E — Has five pieces in a basket.

M 220 A B C — Has the P 192 A & B in the small Oval Woven Basket.

M 221 A B C D — This is M 101 A B C in the large Oval Woven Basket.

M 226 A B C — Made up of M 36 A & B in the small Oval Woven Basket. $55.00

M 227 A B C — This is M 100 B & C in the small Oval Woven Basket. $40.00

M 229 A B C — Includes P 191 A & B in the small Oval Woven Basket. $30.00

M 228 A B C D — Has S 270 Mustard and P 191 A & B in the Long Woven Basket. $42.00

M 235 A B C — Has P 151 A & B in the large Oval Woven Basket. $23.00

M 236 A B C — Consists of M 107 B & C
in the small Oval Woven Basket. $45.00

M 238 A B C — Has P 196 A & B in the medium Oval Woven
Basket. $60.00

M 237 A B C D — This is M 107 A B C in
the Triangle Woven Basket. $90.00

M 240 A B C D — Consists of M 106 A B C Cow
Condiment in the Triangle Woven Basket. $75.00

M 241 A B C — Consists of M 106 B & C in the small Oval Woven Basket. $48.00

M 250 A B C D — Has the P 200 A & B Shakers combined with S 224 in the Plastic Triangle Basket. $38.00

M 251 A B C — Made up of P 200 A & B in the small Plastic Oval Basket. $22.00

M 242 A B C D — Has M 100 A B C in the Triangle Woven Basket. $95.00

M 252 A B C D — Has the 2 Kg. Mustard Pot and 5 Kg. Salt & Pepper Shakers in the Triangle Woven Basket. Rare. $95.00

M 253 A B C — Consists of the 5 Kg. Salt & Pepper Shakers in the small Oval Woven Basket. Scarce. $75.00

M 254 A B C — This is M 2 A Mustard Pot by Karl Simon in 1934 with P 420/0 Salt and P 420/2/0 Pepper by Reinhold Unger in 1927, with no tray. $78.00

M 263 A B C D — Made up of M 116 A B C in the Triangle Woven Basket. $45.00

M 264 A B C — This is M 116 A B C without the tray. $30.00

M 265 A B C — Consists of the P 153 I & O Friars in the small Oval Woven Basket. $23.00

M 281 A B C — Condiment Set.

M 282 A B C — Consists of the three piece Lighthouse. $65.00

M 283 — is a ONE PIECE Salt & Pepper Shaker.

M 288 — Mustard Base Parrot with a Salt AND Pepper Shaker top. The number shown on this and SEVERAL other similar sets is "DRGM 939536". $200.00

M 289 — Mustard Based pair of Ducks with a Salt AND Pepper Shaker top. $200.00

M 291 — Fat Duck with a Mustard Base, Ceramic Spoon, and Shaker top. It was created in 1926, most likely by Max Pechtold. $150.00

M 292 — Swan with a Mustard bottom and a Shaker top.

M 293 — Rabbit with a Mustard bottom, Ceramic Spoon, and Shaker top. 125.00

M 300 A B C D — Stylized Chickens on the M 59 D Tray. $95.00

M 301 A B C D — Consists of M 86 A B C on a Long Tray.

M 302 A B C D — Consists of M 96 A B C on a Long Tray.

M 311 — Consists of M 100 B & C on a Tray.

M 294 — Young Bird with a Mustard Pot bottom, Shaker top, and Ceramic Spoon, created by Max Pechtold in 1926. $125.00

M 295 — Owl with a Mustard Pot base and Shaker top.

M 297 A B C — Has a Toilet for the Mustard Pot with Salt & Pepper.

M 298 — Race Car Condiment Set has a Condiment Pot base and Shaker top.

M 299 — Duck with a Mustard Pot base and Shaker top.

The series of numbers jumps from M 311 to M 341 here. This most likely represents lost records.

The Erect Duck "stretching his neck" is one of the sets with a Mustard Pot base and a Shaker top that most likely falls into this numbering gap. It has the incised "Crown" mark, but no other numbers. Since Goebel cannot identify it by number, I have included it here between M 312 and M 341.

M 340 — This is the number that we "assigned" to this Condiment Set. The Duck has the "Crown" mark, but NO number. Rare. $400.00

M 341 — Pony with a Mustard base and Shaker top.

M 342 — Sitting Pig Condiment Set has a Mustard base, Ceramic Spoon, and Shaker top.

M 346 — Small Round Duckling has a Mustard Pot base, Ceramic Spoon and Shaker top. $100.00

M 343 —Duck with a Topknot has a Mustard Pot base, Ceramic Spoon, and Shaker top. $100.00

M 347 — Floppy Eared Rabbit with left ear down is typical of those sets with a Condiment base, Ceramic Spoon, and Shaker top. Unique. $150.00

M 344 —Parrot sitting on a Cage with a Mustard Pot base, Ceramic Spoon, and Shaker top. $150.00

M 348 — Clown with Mustard Pot base, Ceramic Spoon, and Shaker top. Unique $1,000.00 to $1,500.00

51

M 349 — Owl Condiment with Spoon and Shaker Top.

M 381 A B C — Made up of P 377 large Chick Salt, P 446 small Bird Pepper, and S 584 Condiment Pot, all by Max Mueller in the early 1920s. Unusual. $96.00

M 353 A B C D — Has a Mustard Pot and P 657 I & O Shakers by Lofl, sitting on a tray designed by Max Kohles, all created in 1928. Unique. $75.00 to $125.00

M 382 A B C — Consists of S 600 Condiment Pot, P 601 Salt, and P 602 Pepper, by Max Pechtold in 1927. Notice that the spoon is also one of the Mustard's trunks. No tray is assigned to this scarce set. $100.00

M 355 A B C D — Cow Condiment Set sculpted by Max Pechtold in 1927. Scarce. $100.00 to $125.00

M 391 A B C — Dog Condiment Set with no assigned Tray, has S 601 Mustard combined with P 435/0 and P 435/2/0 Salt & Pepper. Theo Menzenbach sculpted the wistful Dachshunds. $125.00

M 377 — Open Salters and Mustard Pot.

M 392 A B C — Duck Condiment Set with P 490 Salt Shaker and Duck Pepper Shaker.

M 393 A B C — Buzzard or Pelican Condiment Pot and Shakers.

M 394 A B C — Stork Mustard Pot and Stork Shakers.

M 395 A B C —Rabbit Condiment Pot, by Max Pechtold in 1927, combined with P 387/0 Salt Shaker by Arthur Moeller in 1923, and P 473 Pepper Shaker by Max Kohles in 1926. $75.00

M 396 A B C — Sitting Pigs Condiment and Shakers.

M 397 A B C — Consists of S 588 Duck Mustard Pot with P 490 Salt & P 411 Pepper Shakers.

M 398 Dep — Has a Rabbit Salt Dip and a Pepper Shaker.

M 401 A B C D — This is set M 381 A B C on a tray.

M 402 A B C D — This is set M 382 A B C on a tray.

M 403 A B C — Rabbits in a deep tray with a center handle.

M 404 A B C — Chicks in a deep tray with a center handle.

M 405 A B C — Rabbits in a tray.

M 407 A B C — Rabbit Shakers in a deep tray with a Mustard Pot.

M 408 A B C — Elephant Shakers in a deep tray with a Mustard Pot.

M 409 A B C — Barrel shaped Shakers in a deep tray with a Mustard Pot.

M 410 A B C — Shakers in a ceramic basket.

M 411 A B C D — Combines the P 697 and P 704 Soldier Shakers with a Soldier Condiment Pot by Arthur Moeller in 1932, placed on the tray created by Max Pechtold. $95.00

M 412 A B C D — Cylindrical shaped Shakers and Condiment Pot on M 59 D Tray.

M 413 A B C — A Maid holding a serving tray with a pair of Shakers on it.

M 414 A B C — "Eggcup" shaped Shakers and Mustard Pot.

M 415 A B C — Consists of M 395 A B C on a tray.

M 424 A B C D — P 636 Salt Shaker and P 637 Pepper Shaker goes with S 610 Condiment and Ceramic Spoon on the M 355 D Tray. Rare. $250.00

M 419 A B C D E F —Five pieces in an extra long Metal Basket. This is quite similar to M 428, except it also has matching Oil and Vinegar bottles and a longer basket. The long basket is RARE! $100.00+

M 428 A B C D — Consists of M 114 A B C in the long Metal Basket. Scarce basket. $65.00 to $100.00

M 421 A B C D — Consists of M 381 A B C positioned on the M 355 D Tray. $120.00 to $140.00

M 429 A B C — Consists of P 191 A & B Shakers in the Oval Metal Basket. Scarce basket. $85.00

M 435 A B C D — Consists of M 395 on a tray.

---

MAR 804 A B C D — Crook Salt, Cop Pepper, and Judge Condiment Pot on T 76 Tray designed by Naumann and Karl Wagner in 1958. Scarce. $150.00 to $200.00.

MAR 805 A B C —Clown Salt, Stylized Cat Pepper, and Tray T 71/0, all created by Karl Wagner and Naumann in 1958. $75.00

MAR 806 — Has a Ghost as the Salt Shaker, and an Owl as the Pepper Shaker. Naumann and Karl Wagner placed the pair on tray T 71/0 when they finished the design. $75.00

MAR 807 A B C — A pair that has names. "Kochin Berta" (Cook Berta) is the three-hole Salt Shaker and "Soldat Horn" (Soldier Bugle) has two holes as the Pepper Shaker. Naumann and Karl Wagner did the shakers and the set was issued on Tray T 71/0. $75.00

M/GRA 231 A B C D — Comprised of GRA 109 with the Bountiful pattern, in the Triangle Woven Basket. $45.00

M/GRA 232 A B C — This is the GRA 109 B & C Salt & Pepper Shakers in the Medium Oval Woven Basket. $30.00

M/GRA 244 A B C — Has GRA 123 Fox and Vixen Shakers in the small Oval Woven Basket. $100.00

M/GRA 245 A B C — Includes GRA 124 A & B Shakers in the small Oval Woven Basket.

M/GRA 243 A B C — Made up of GRA 125 A & B Rabbits Salt & Pepper Shakers in the small Oval Woven Basket. $100.00

M/GRA 247 A B C — Consists of GRA 127 Man and Woman in the small Oval Woven Basket. $100.00

M/GRA 248 A B C — Has GRA 128 A & B Salt & Pepper Shakers in the small Oval Woven Basket. $100.00

M/GRA 260 A B C D — Made up of GRA 147 Salt & Pepper Shakers and GRA 148 Condiment Pot in the Triangle Plastic Basket. $95.00

M/GRA 249 A B C — Comprised of GRA 129 A & B in the small Oval Woven Basket. $100.00

M/GRA 261 — This is the small Plastic Basket containing GRA 147 A & B Salt & Pepper Shakers. $70.00

57

M/GRA 266 — Made up of GRA 204 A B C in the Plastic Triangle Basket. $80.00

M/GRA 278 A B C — Made up of GRA 195 A & B Rooster Shakers in the large Plastic Oval Basket. $50.00

M/GRA 267 — This is just GRA 204 A & B in the small Plastic Oval Basket. $50.00

M/GRA 271 A B C D E F G — Has GRA 179 A & B Shakers plus five other pieces in a basket built for seven objects.

M/GRA 272 A B C D E — Has GRA 179 A & B Shakers and four other pieces in a basket built for six.

M/GRA 277 A B C — Consists of GRA 197 A & B Bird Salt & Pepper Shakers in the large Plastic Oval Basket. $35.00

M/GRA 431 A B C D — Consists of GRA 109 A B C in the long Metal Basket. Basket is scarce. $55.00 to $75.00

M/GRA 432 A B C — Comprised of GRA 109 B & C in the Oval Metal Basket for two pieces. Basket is scarce. $50.00 to $70.00

M/GRA 441 A B C D — Has GRA 176 Condiment Pot, GRA 179 A Salt Shaker and GRA 179 B Pepper Shaker in the long Metal Basket.

M/GRA 442 A B C — Consists of GRA 179 A & B Salt & Pepper Shakers in the Oval Metal Basket. $50.00 to $70.00

NA 32 A & B — A pair of Rabbit Heads that Helmuth Wehlte sculpted from the artwork of "Nasha" in 1956. $50.00 to 70.00

NA 34 — A set comprised of NA 32 A & B Salt & Pepper Shakers on M 42 D Tray along with a Rabbit Faced Egg Cup.

P 1 — Sitting Rabbit as a Shaker, 1934.

P 2 — Rabbit as a Shaker, 1934.

P 3 — Pear as a Shaker.

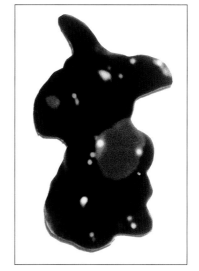

P 4 — Dog holding a Heart Salt Shaker, created by Reinhold Unger in 1934. Scarce. $25.00 single.

P 5 — Dog holding a
Clover Flower Pepper
Shaker, by Reinhold Unger
in 1934. Scarce. $25.00
single.

P 6 — Dog holding a Mushroom,
by Reinhold Unger in 1934. Scarce.
$25.00 single.

P 7 — Sitting Bear, sculpted by Arthur Moeller.

P 8 — Cylindrical with Six Ribs Shaker, by Max Kohles in 1935.

P 9 — Apple as a Shaker, by Erich Popp in 1935.

P 10 — Pear as a Shaker, by Erich Popp in 1935.

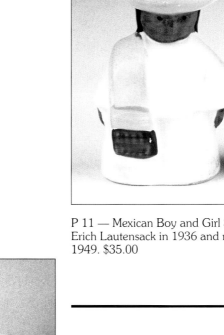

P 11 — Mexican Boy and Girl Salt & Pepper, originally shaped by
Erich Lautensack in 1936 and re-sculpted by Reinhold Unger in
1949. $35.00

P 12 A & B — Crawfish, caught by Erich Lautensack in 1936.

P 13 — Flower, grown by Erich Lautensack in 1936.

P 14 — Sitting Chick, hatched by Erich Popp in 1936.

P 15 — Daisy with Petals Down, planted by Reinhold Unger in
1936.

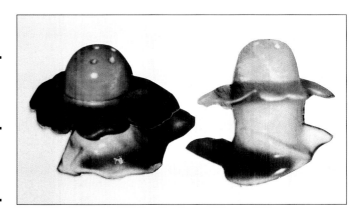

P 16 — Narcissus Flower with Petals Down,
by Reinhold Unger in 1936. $70.00

P 17 — Daisy with Petals Up by Reinhold Unger in 1936. $70.00

P 18 and P 19 — Tyrol Boy as Salt and Tyrol Girl as a Pepper, by Erich Lautensack in 1936. $18.00 to $20.00

P 20 A & B — Holland Boy and Girl Salt & Pepper by Erich Lautensack in 1936 has the normal seven and five hole pre-WW II pattern. Re-sculpted by Arthur Moeller in 1949 with the typical post-war hole pattern of three for the salt and two for the pepper. $20.00 / pair

P 21 Rooster and P 22 Hen — Hatched by Erich Lautensack in 1936.

P 23 — Pickwick as a Salt Shaker, by Unkauft in 1936 and re-sculpted by Arthur Moeller in 1949. $20.00 single

P 24 — Sam Weller as a Salt Shaker, by Unkauft in 1936 and re-sculpted by Reinhold Unger in 1949. $20.00 single

P 25 — Bumble as a Salt Shaker, by Unkauft in 1936 and re-sculpted by Reinhold Unger in 1949. $20.00 single

P 26 — Mrs. Gamp as a Pepper Shaker, by Unkauft in 1936 and re-sculpted in 1949 as a pair by Arthur Moeller. $20.00 pre-war single, $35.00 post-war pair.

P 27 A & B — Boy with a Concertina as Salt and Girl with a Parasol as Pepper, by Theo Menzenbach in 1949. $35.00

P 28 — Boy, by Arthur Moeller in 1936.

P 29 — Sitting Girl with a large Hat, by Moeller in 1936.

P 30 — Girl Skier standing and holding skis, by Moeller in 1936. $40.00 single

P 31 — Girl, by Arthur Moeller.

P 32 — Construction Worker holding an Umbrella, by Reinhold Unger in 1936, has no specific mate. Shown are one with a pre-war hole pattern and one with a post-war pattern. $35.00 each

P 35 — Construction Worker playing a Concertina by Reinhold Unger in 1936. The right hand one has the post-war hole pattern. $35.00 each

P 33 — Construction Worker holding Flowers, by Reinhold Unger in 1936. Pre-war on the left. $35.00 each

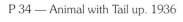

P 34 — Animal with Tail up. 1936

P 36 A & B — Norwegian Boy Salt and Girl Pepper Shakers carved by Reinhold Unger in 1936. $30.00

P 37/I A & B — Holland Boy and Girl dressed by Erich Lautensack in 1937. Note the pre-war hole pattern.

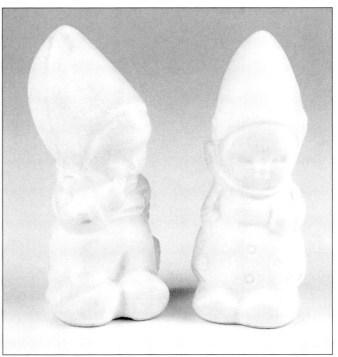

P 37/0 — A post-war set in white glaze.

P 38 and P 39 — Heart with an Edelweiss Flower on it (P 38) and Heart with a Flower on it (P 39), contrived by Moeller in 1937.

P 40 A & B — Ducks.

P 41 A & B — Man and Woman (perhaps depicting Charlie Chaplin and Myrna Loy), arranged by Erich Lautensack in 1937.

P 37/0 — Post-war style with three holes for the Salt and two holes for the Pepper. $28.00 / pair

P 42 A & B — Sitting Boy and Girl, by Arthur Moeller in 1937. $45.00

P 43 — Light House, by Erich Lautensack in 1937.

P 44 — This is a series of birds attributed to Ynkauft, which means literally "Traveling Salesman" in German. We presume that it indicates an itinerant artist. This one was made as a pair, and is P 44/0 A & E Red Birds. $45.00

P 44/0 C — A Red Bird facing left. $25.00 each single

P 44/0 A & E — The same pair of P 44/0 A & E in Green. $45.00 pair

P 44/0 B — Has a short beak and its head is down. $25.00 single

P 44/0 D — A Blue and Yellow Parakeet. $25.00 single

P 44/0 F — Has a long bill. $25.00 single

P 48 — Probably paired with P 47 and has a Rabbit emerging. Scarce. $50.00

P 44/A/0 — Has red around its beak. $25.00 single

P 49 and P 50— Dog with a Base Fiddle (P 49) pairs with Dog with a Concertina (P 50), by Reinhold Unger in 1938. $40.00

P 45 A & B — Boy and Girl holding Grapes, by Moeller in 1937.

P 51 — Dog with a Flute, by Reinhold Unger in 1938.

P 46 — Pine Tree, by Erich Lautensack in 1937.

P 52 — Barrel Salt Shaker with writing on it, by Reinhold Unger in 1939.

P 53 — Barrel pairs with P 52, and says Limburger on it. Also by Reinhold Unger.

P 47 — A Chick emerging from an Egg.

The following series of girls with odd hats was created by Reinhold Unger in 1945, and was an early attempt to get Goebel back into production, in peacetime. The first pieces were made with the pre-war hole pattern of seven for the Salt and five for the Pepper. These pieces also have unusual coloring, as materials were scarce right after World War II. Soon the colors got better, and the hole patterns were switched to the typical post-war pattern of three holes for the Salt and two holes for the Pepper.

P 56 — Girl with Rose as a Hat, Salt Shaker. $25.00 each

P 54 — Girl with Dahlia as a Hat, Salt Shaker. The left hand shakers in this series have pre-war hole patterns. $25.00 each

P 55 — Girl with Sunflower as a Hat, Pepper Shaker. The series was intended to be mixed and matched. $25.00 each

P 57 — Girl with Strawberry as a Hat, Salt Shaker. $25.00 each

P 58 — Girl with Raspberry as a Hat, Pepper Shaker. $25.00 each

P 60 — Girl with Plum as a Hat, Pepper Shaker. Note the off color of the early plum, on the left. $25.00 each

P 59 — Girl with Apple as a Hat, Salt Shaker. $25.00 each

P 62 — Girl with Pansy as a Hat, Pepper Shaker. $25.00 each

---

P 61 B & C — Vases with Flowers, designed by Arthur Moeller in 1946; shown as part of M 24 Condiment Set.

---

P 63 —Rococo Little Girl holding a Fan in her right hand, worked out by Reinhold Unger in 1949.

P 64 — Little Girl with Umbrella in her right hand, contrived by Reinhold Unger in 1949.

P 67 A & B — Stacking Hen Pepper on Basket Salt Shaker, created by Reinhold Unger in 1949. $35.00

P 65 — Standing Black Boy with both hands on his belly. He wears bones all around his waist. Reinhold Unger first saw this cannibal in 1949. $60.00 two

P 66 A & B — Stacking Chick Pepper on Egg Salt Shaker, sculpted by Reinhold Unger in 1949. $35.00

P 68 — Stacking Holland Girl. The top half is a Pepper Shaker, and the lower section is for Salt. Reinhold Unger created her too, in 1949. $38.00

P 69 A & B — Large and Small Chimney Sweeps, dusted of by Arthur Moeller in 1949. Scarce. $75.00

P 70 — Chinese Temple built by A. Moeller in 1949.

P 71 A & B — Chinese Boy Salt and Girl Holding a Fan Pepper, arranged by Arthur Moeller in 1949. $55.00

P 72 — Chinese, schemed up by Arthur Moeller in 1949.

P 73 — Mushroom with little Mushrooms at the base, carved by Reinhold Unger in 1949.

P 74 and P 75 — Pig with a Base Fiddle (P 74) and Pig with a Drum (P 75). Erich Popp sculpted these pink pigs in 1949. $40.00

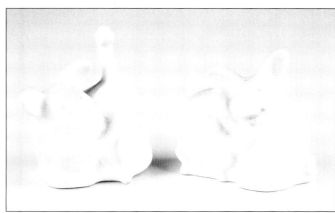

P 74 and P 75 —The Pigs are also available in a dull white glaze. $40.00

P 76 A & B — Drake Salt and Duck Pepper Shakers. Hatched and formed by Theo Menzenbach in 1949. $20.00

P 77 A & B — Pheasant Salt & Pepper Shakers, contrived by Theo Menzenbach in 1949. $20.00

P 78 A & B — Flamingo Salt & Pepper Shakers, colored by Theo Menzenbach in 1949. $25.00

P 79 A & B — Tom Turkey Salt Shaker and Hen Turkey Pepper Shaker, by master sculptor Theo Menzenbach in mid century. $22.00

P 80 A & B — Pheasants. A is the Salt Shaker, with tail feathers up, formatted by Theo Menzenbach in 1950.

---

P 81 A & B — Chicken Pheasants, planned by Theo Menzenbach in 1950.

---

P 82 A & B — Quail, by Theo Menzenbach in 1950 (may have been the "model" for P 125).

---

P 85 A & B — English Soldiers, marched into existence by Theo Menzenbach in 1950. $45.00

P 83 — Salt Shaker Cat with Tail Up, thought up by Theo Menzenbach in 1950. Scarce. $100.00

The next group of shakers are "Hugging and Kissing." Arthur Moeller and Reinhold Unger probably had a friendly competition with the series, in 1950. In each case the Boy is the Salt shaker with three holes in the head, and the Girl is the Pepper with two holes on the top of the head.

P 84 A & B — Owls Sitting on Books, read by Reinhold Unger in 1950. Scarce. $75.00

P 86 A & B — Cowboy and Cowgirl Kissers, planned by A. Moeller. $70.00

P 87 A & B — Indian Boy and Girl Huggers, accomplished by Reinhold Unger. $70.00

P 89 A & B — Dressed up Southern Couple Kissers, thought up by A. Moeller. $75.00

P 88 A & B — Chinese Boy and Girl Huggers, shaped by Arthur Moeller. $70.00

P 90 A & B — Scotty Dog Huggers, raised by Arthur Moeller in 1950. $65.00

P 91 A & B — Pigs Hugging, slopped by Moeller. The one looking right has three holes for the Salt. $60.00

P 93 A & B — Hollanders that Hug, produced by Reinhold Unger. $65.00

P 92 A & B — African Boy and Girl Kissers, by Reinhold Unger. $150.00

P 94 A & B — Cats that sit up and kiss, designed by Reinhold Unger. $60.00

P 96 — Skiing Boy and Girl without a hat on the Girl.

P 95 A & B — Chef and Cook fool around in the kitchen, contrived by Arthur Moeller. $60.00

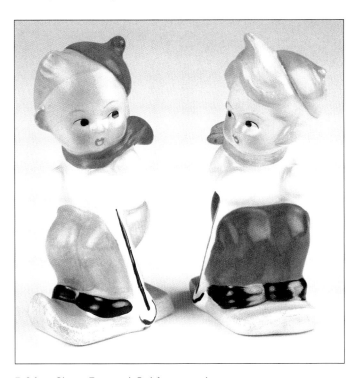

P 96 — Skiing Boy and Girl facing each other, by Arthur Moeller in 1950. $65.00

P 97 A & B — Tyrolean Boy and Girl Huggers, by Reinhold Unger, also in 1950. $65.00

P 98 A & B — Sprinkling Cans, tinkered with by Reinhold Unger in 1950. $22.00

P 99 A & B — Kegler Salt Shaker and King Pin Pepper Shaker. Arthur Moeller was bowled over when he thought them up in 1950. The Pin is scarce. $400.00

P 100 — Chicken on an oval base, Pepper Shaker, by Ferendes Lauslo in 1950.

P 101/0 A & B — "Plymouth Rock" Chickens, hatched by Ferendes Lauslo in 1950. $35.00

P 101/1 A & B — "Rhode Island Red" Chickens, designed by Ferendes Lauslo in 1950. $35.00

P 102 & P 103 — Red Pepper Salt Shaker (P 102) and Green Pepper two-hole Pepper Shaker (P 103), raised by Ferendes Lauslo in 1950. $28.00

P 104 A & B — Pumpkin Shaped Zucchini, thought up by Ferendes Lauslo in 1950. $30.00

P 105 & P 106— Mushroom Salt (P105) and Frog Pepper (P 106), by Karl Wagner in 1950. $28.00

P 107 A & B — Scottish Terrier (A) and Skye Terrier (B), sculpted by Arthur Moeller in 1950. $38.00

P 108 A & B — Pots for Coffee, perked in 1950 by Theo Menzenbach. $22.00

P 110 A & B — Man with a High Hat Salt and Girl in a Bonnet as Pepper, dressed by Reinhold Unger in 1950. Scarce. $95.00

P 109 A & B — Bashful Tyroleans, introduced by Arthur Moeller in 1950. $38.00

P 111 A & B — Native Serenading his Girl with a Mandolin. Music by Karl Wagner, in 1950. $200.00

P 112 A & B — Mushroom Stacking Set, with the top as the Pepper Shaker. Fungus gathered by Karl Wagner in 1950.

P 113 — Stork standing on a nest, created by Reinhold Unger in 1950.

P 116 A & B — Squirrel Salt and Acorn Pepper, planted by Karl Wagner in 1950. $24.00

P 114 A & B — Wild Turkey Pepper Shaker stacked on a Nest Salt Shaker, incubated by Karl Wagner in 1950. $22.00

P 115 A & B — Rabbit Salt Shaker holding a Carrot Pepper Shaker, arranged by Karl Wagner in 1950. $30.00

P 117 A & B — Coffee Pot and Tea Pot, formed by Wagner in 1951. $18.00

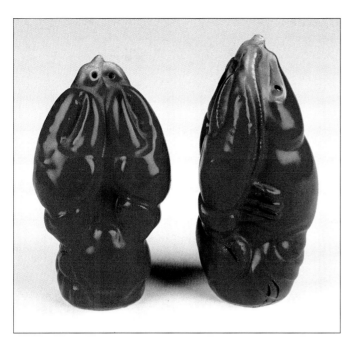

P 118 A & B — Lobsters with three and two holes Salt & Pepper, caught by Karl Wagner. $33.00

P 119 A & B — Chipmunk with a Nut Salt Shaker and Chipmunk on all Fours as Pepper Shaker. Karl Wagner did them in 1951. $35.00

P 120 A & B — Skunk Salt & Pepper, by Karl Wagner in 1951. $65.00

P 121 A & B — Pekingese Dog Salt & Pepper Shakers, thought up by Karl Wagner in 1951. $25.00

P 122 A & B — Goose Pepper Shaker on a Platter Salt Shaker, by Karl Wagner in 1951.

P 123 A & B — Boy and Girl Holding Grapes, pressed by Karl Wagner in 1951. $35.00

P 124 A & B — Turkey Pepper Shaker stacked on a Nest Salt Shaker. In my opinion, this is identical to P 114, and probably someone mis-numbered a master mold. Attributed to Karl Wagner in 1951. $22.00

P 128 A & B — A is the Salt and has the right hand on his chin. B is the Pepper and has the left hand on her stomach. Karl Wagner monkeyed around with these too, in 1951. $38.00

P 125 A & B — Quail, hatched by Karl Wagner in 1951. $15.00

P 126 A & B — Sitting Monkeys. A is the Salt Shaker and has the hand on his stomach. B has the left hand out. Karl Wagner did these in 1951.

P 129 A & B — Zebra. The translation calls them "Sitting Zebra," but the only examples to surface are the two identical, three-hole standing Salt Shakers shown. Hans Zetzmann painted the stripes in 1951. Rare. $100.00

P 127 A & B — Rooster with three holes and Hen with two, for the Pepper. Hans Zetzmann whipped them up in 1950. $22.00

P 130 A & B — Kissing Bride and Groom, married by Karl Wagner in 1951. $40.00

P 131 A & B — Standing Bride and
Groom, just married by Karl Wagner, one
year after the mid century. $40.00

P 132 — Standing Man.

P 135 A & B — Alpine Boy and Girl,
scaled by Karl Wagner in 1952. $45.00

P 136 A & B — Pelicans. Karl Wagner fed them fish in 1952.

P 133 A & B — Rabbits with Twisted Ears. The
hares' ears were tied by Arthur Moeller in 1951.
$75.00

P 134 A & B — Holland Boy Salt and Girl Pepper
Shakers, dressed by Karl Wagner in 1952. $40.00

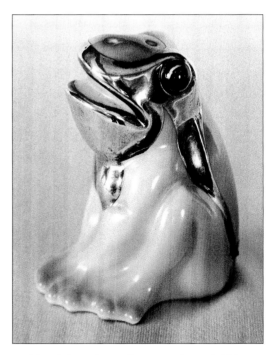

P 137 A & B — Sitting Frogs, similar to P 380.
Tadpoles by Karl Wagner in 1952. $30.00

P 138 A & B — Black Forest Boy and Girl, shaped by Hans Zetzmann in 1952. $38.00

P 139 — Snail, two-hole Pepper Shaker with the three-hole Shell on his back as Salt, designed by Karl Wagner in 1952. $29.00

P 140 — Vase, contrived by Franz Barth in 1953.

P 141 A & B — Large and Small Seahorses, sculpted by Hans Zetzmann in 1953. $55.00

P 142 A & B — Chianti Bottles, emptied by Kuhn in 1953. $15.00

P 143 & P 144 — Standing Cow as a Salt Shaker (P143) and Lying Cow as a Pepper Shaker (P 144), created by Arthur Moeller in 1953.

P 145 A & B — Standing Pigs.

P 146 — Sitting Dog with two holes as a Pepper Shaker, arranged by Arthur Moeller in 1953.

P 147 — Horse with two holes as a Pepper Shaker, schemed up by Moeller in 1953.

P 148 — Elephant Sitting Erect as a three-hole Salt Shaker, carved by Arthur Moeller in 1953.

P 149 A & B — Girls with Large Hats, formed by Moeller in 1953. $39.00

P 150 A & B — Carp. Hans Zetzmann
fished these up in 1953. $18.00

P 152 A & B — Laughing Rabbits, carved
by Arthur Moeller in 1953. $38.00

P 151 A & B — White Poodle for Salt and Black
Poodle for Pepper. It was 1953 when Arthur Moeller
whipped these up. $19.00

P 153/0 — Friar Tuck, same size, three and two holes. First
created by Reinhold Unger in 1954, with sandals on and toes
exposed. By 1955, the toes disappeared. Scarce with toes
exposed. $35.00

P 151 A & B — The Poodles in pink. $19.00

P 153 I & O — Large and Small Friars with
toes exposed, 1954. $35.00

P 153/0 — Friars, same size with toes exposed, in white glazed finish. Scarce. $45.00

P 153 A & B — Changed in 1955 to "Black Shoes." They were issued in this version, and also two the same size. These versions were produced until 1989 so the supply is "plentiful." $15.00 to $25.00

P 153/0 — Special Friar. A Goebel master painter hand painted the face for us. Unique.

P 154 A & B — Bear Salt Shaker and Beehive Pepper Shaker, formatted by Karl Wagner and Schumann in 1954. $20.00

P 153 A & B — Cardinal Tuck, released in 1960 in Europe, then released in the US in 1963, but discontinued in 1965. Scarce. $125.00 to $150.00

P 156 A & B — Rabbit Salt Shaker and Cabbage Pepper Shaker, accomplished by Karl Wagner in 1954. (Note: this Rabbit is often confused with one of the Laughing Rabbits.) $30.00

P 154 A & B — Bear and Beehive set in white glaze. $20.00

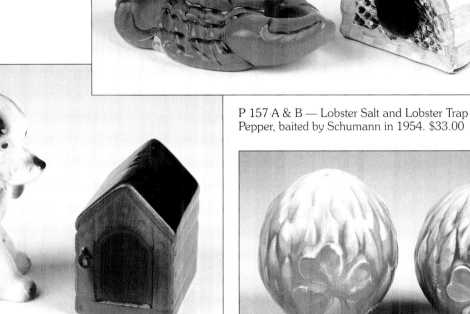

P 157 A & B — Lobster Salt and Lobster Trap Pepper, baited by Schumann in 1954. $33.00

P 155 A & B — Big Dog and a Little Doghouse, planned (but not too well, as the dog does not fit in the house) by Karl Wagner in 1954. $28.00

P 158 A & B — Clover Flowers, grown by Karl Wagner in 1954. $25.00

P 159 A & B — Corn on the Cob. Karl Wagner produced the large one for the Salt and the small one for the Pepper in 1954. $38.00

P 160 A & B — Eggs with Faces sticking out one "END." Karl Wagner hatched this idea in 1954. $40.00

P 161 — Mushroom Salt Shaker with three holes and a Gnome's face showing.

P 162 — Mushroom Pepper Shaker with two holes and a Gnome's face showing.

P 163 A & B — Salt & Pepper Hares with a Golf Club and a Cricket Bat, played by Helmuth Wehlte in 1956. $55.00

P 164 A & B — Rabbits with Edelweiss Flowers in their mouths, designed by Ewald Wolf in 1956. $45.00

P 165 A & B — Stacking Flower Pepper Shaker on the Salt Flower Pot, planted by Wagner and Thubner in 1956. $40.00

P 166 A & B — Elephants. B, the Pepper Shaker holds the tail of A with its trunk. Helmuth Wehlte taught them the trick in 1956. $55.00

P 167 A & B — French Style Telephone, with the receiver as a Pepper Shaker on the Salt base, called up by Thubner in 1956. Scarce. $59.00

P 168 A & B — Sitting Camel Salt Shaker reclining next to a sitting Arab Pepper Shaker, by Helmuth Wehlte in 1956. $60.00

P 169 A & B — Swedish Boy and Girl, dressed by Karl Wagner in 1956. $55.00

P 170 A & B — Sitting Bear Salt & Pepper Shakers, hunted by Karl Wagner in 1956. $125.00

P 172 A & B — Sitting Boxer Dog Shakers. Karl Wagner kept the ears up on the Salt Shaker and ears down on the Pepper, in 1957. $70.00

P 171 A & B — Sitting Kitten Salt & Pepper Shakers, by Karl Wagner in 1956. $33.00

P 173 A & B — Rugby Player Salt Shaker and Rugby Ball Pepper Shaker, kicked off by Helmuth Wehlte in 1957. $65.00

P 174 A & B — Black Children, only produced as a sample, by Reinhold Unger in 1957.

P 176 A & B — Cardinal Tuck carrying Books. $125.00

P 175 A & B — Night Watchmen, by Wagner.
The 1957 larger one is the Salt Shaker. $69.00

P 176 A & B — Friar Tuck carrying Books,
by Theo Menzenbach in 1957. $45.00

P 177 A & B — Young Boys, modeled after the Belgian statue "Pis," by K. Wagner in 1958. Scarce. $85.00

P 178 A & B — Owls. The Salt as designed in 1958 by Helmuth Wehlte has the wings down, while the Pepper has its wings spread. $65.00

P 179 A & B — Cats with Nylon Whiskers. The white Salt Shaker looks left, while the black Pepper Shaker looks right. Arthur Moeller did them in 1959. $29.00

P 180 A & B — These Shakers are the first of three consecutive pairs of "Natural Enemies." A, the Salt, is a Stylized Duck while B is a Stylized Fox. $125.00

P 181 A & B — Stylized Cat and Stylized Dog, by Gerhard Skrobek. $175.00

P 182 A & B — Stylized Seal and Stylized Penguin, created in 1959. $200.00

P 184 A & B — Kittens, A with an Apron and B with a Bib, sculpted by Marianne Brandl, in 1960. $25.00

P 184 A & B were also issued in these unusual colors. $30.00

P 183 A & B — Small Clowns, by Gerhard Skrobek in 1959. $65.00

P 185 A & B — Stacking Mouse as the Salt Shaker with a cylindrical Base as the Pepper Shaker, by Naumann in 1960. $39.00

P 186 — Kitten Salt holding a Ball as the Pepper Shaker, planned by Naumann in 1960. $45.00

P 188 — Mushrooms, by Karl Wagner in 1960.

P 189 A & B — Friar Tuck. The one playing the flute is the Salt Shaker. $90.00

P 190 A & B — Eggs. The yellow one has three holes as a Salt Shaker and the blue one has two holes for the Pepper. Gerhard Skrobek "laid" these out in 1961. Scarce. $45.00

P 191 A & B — Striped Oval Shakers, 2-1/2" tall, molded by Gerhard Skrobek in 1962. $22.00

P 192 A & B — Stylized Owls. Whoo made them? Horst Aschermann, in 1962.

P 193 A & B — Lucerne Switzerland Water Towers, constructed by Wolfgang Ebert in 1962. $65.00

P 194 A & B — Cactus with faces, by Gerhard Skrobek in 1962.

P 195 A & B — Ducks sitting erect. The female has a top knot, is larger, and is the Salt Shaker. Created by Karl Wagner in 1962. $50.00

P 196 A & B — Pigs sitting erect and named "Lucky Chap," propped up by Wolfgang Ebert in 1962. $45.00

P 197 — Penguins, by Oskar Hoernlein in 1963. $29.00

P 198 A & B — Ducks in an Egg, by Gerhard Skrobek in 1963.

P 199 A & B — One piece Shaker, created by Gerhard Skrobek in 1963.

94

P 200 A & B — Mushrooms, by Gerhard Skrobek in 1963. $23.00

P 202 A & B — Stylized Birds, contrived
by Wolfgang Ebert in 1966. $65.00

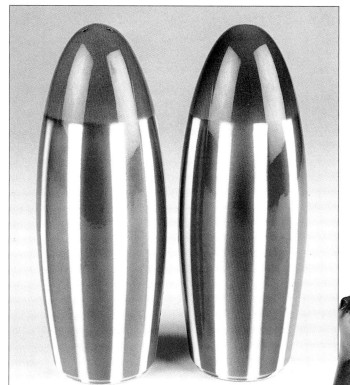

P 201 A & B — Tall Oval pair worked out
by Arthur Moeller in 1964. $24.00

P 203 A & B — Playful Ducks, sculpted by Gerhard Skrobek in
1966.

P 204 A & B — Cone Shaped Shakers, created by Wolfgang Ebert
in 1967.

P 205 A & B — Ducks.

P 206 A & B — Sea Lions. Skrobek had nothing better to do in
1967, so he drilled three holes in the gray one for Salt, and two
holes in the green one for Pepper. $30.00

P 209 A & B — Spaniel Dogs with the same pose, arranged by Gerhard Skrobek in 1967. $29.00

P 207 A & B — Penguins, created by Gerhard Skrobek in 1967. The three-hole Shaker is for Salt. $70.00

P 210 A & B — Corgi Dogs sitting erect, formed by Gerhard Skrobek in 1967. $33.00

P 208 A & B — Standing Kittens, by Gerhard Skrobek in 1967. They would be identical except the Salt has one more hole than the Pepper. $29.00

P 211 A & B — Sitting Scottish Terriers, by Gerhard Skrobek in 1967. $27.00

P 212 — Pigs.

P 213 A & B — Gray-Brown Swallows, 1970. $30.00

P 213 A & B — The Swallows in blue. $30.00

There is a large gap in the Goebel numbering system between P 213 and P 371. The dates of manufacture are not logically in order, as P 371 goes back to the 1920s.

P 371 — Shaker.

P 372 — 3" tall Cylinder with Salz on it, and a 3-1/2" tall one with a (Red) Cross and Hygienisch on it.

P 373 I & O — Rabbits.

P 375 — Bird, formed by Arthur Moeller in 1927. Rare. $100.00 one piece.

P 376 — Pair of 2-1/4" tall Cylinders with a (Red) Cross, Hygienisch on one, and Pfeffer on the other.

P 380 I & O — Sitting Frogs, designed by O. Moeller in 1923. $40.00

P 377 — Bird sitting erect, shaped by Arthur Moeller in 1921. Rare. $45.00 for one.

P 381 I & O — Sitting Dogs, worked out by O. Moeller in 1923. $33.00

P 378 I & O — Platypus Salt & Pepper, created by Arthur Moeller in 1921. $35.00 to $50.00

P 379 — Sitting Bear.

P 382 I & O — Cats Sitting and facing right, by Max Moeller about 1924. $25.00

P 383 I & O — Green Owls, by Reinhold Unger in 1924. $50.00

P 385 — Tropical Bird, contrived by Arthur Moeller in 1923. Scarce. $65.00 each

P 383 I & O — Brown Owls. $50.00

P 384 — Standing Duck, created in 1923.

P 386 I & O — Arab, sculpted by Max Moeller in 1924. $80.00 pair

P 387 — Sitting Rabbits with the pre-war hole pattern of seven for Salt and five for the Pepper Shaker, created by Max Moeller, in 1924. $45.00

P 388 — Sitting Rabbit with ears straight up, arranged by Arthur Moeller, in 1924. Scarce. $85.00 to $100.00

P 387 A & B — Post-war Rabbits, $40.00

P 389 — Rabbit Head.

P 387 A & B — Rabbits in Blue. $75.00

P 390 — Elephants with trunks way up. The number P390 is among a group first made in 1924. Scarce. $100.00

P 391 A & B — Dog and Cat. The molds are actually P 381 Dog and P 382 Cat. $35.00 to $50.00

P 391 (conflicting number) — Two attached Bowls.

P 394 I & O — Crouching Kittens with Cloth Tails. Rare. $100.00

P 395 — Rabbit with right ear up and left ear down.

P 396 — Parrots, schemed up by O. Moeller in 1924. Scarce. $100.00

P 397 — Tropical Bird.

P 398 — Boy with a heart on his chest.

P 399 — Girl's Head.

P 400 — Black Boy's Head.

P 407 — Girl's Head wearing a kerchief.

P 412 I & O — Sitting Monkeys, created by Reinhold Unger in 1924. Rare. $100.00+

P 411/0 & P 411/2/0 — Ducks, modeled by Erich Woehner in 1924. $45.00

P 413 I & O —Standing Bears. Ours are only marked BAVARIA. Rare. $135.00 to $150.00

P 411/0 — Post-war pair. $40.00

P 414 I & O — Pelicans, hatched by O. Moeller in 1924 . $50.00

P 415 I & O — Sitting Pigs, conjured up by Max Moeller in 1924.

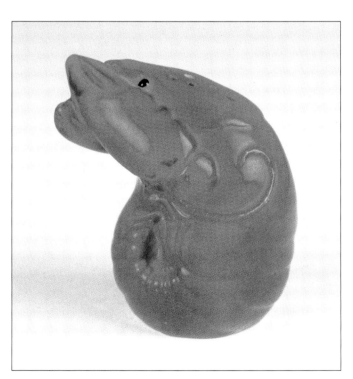

P 416 A & B — Crawfish with seven and five holes.
(The correct pair is scarce.) $90.00 to $100.00 / pair

P 417 — Pear.

P 418 — Mushroom.

P 419 — The translation is "Mascot." The figure has
wings, thus "Guardian Angel." Rare. $150.00 Each

P 420/0 & P 420/2/0 — Large and Small Mushrooms. The fungus
was cultured by Reinhold Unger in 1927. $25.00 to 35.00

P 421 — Buddha.

---

P 422 — Baby's Head.

---

P 423 — Baby Bird, first made in 1924.

---

P 424 — Devil.

---

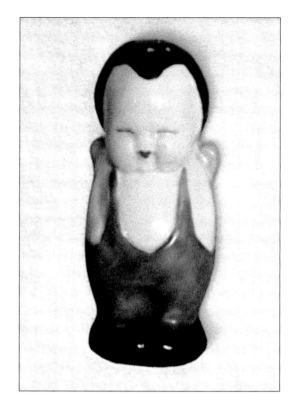

P 428 — Translation is "Mascot" (the figurine has wings); probably more literally "Guardian Angel." Rare. $150.00

---

P 429 — Figurine (could be a bird) wearing a ladies hat.

---

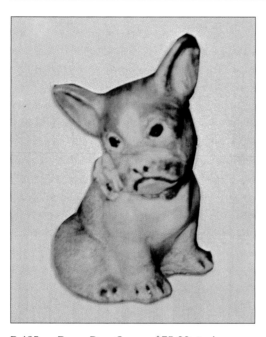

P 425 — Boxer Dog. Scarce. $75.00 single

P 427 — Kitten looking right with right paw up. Scarce. $40.00 single.

P 430 — Sitting Puppy Dog. Scarce. $40.00 single.

P 431 — Chinese Man. Rare. $150.00

P 434 — Raven, carved by O. Moeller in 1924. Scarce. $75.00

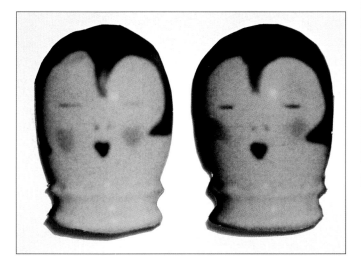

P 432 — Pierrot. $50.00

P 435 — Forlorn Dog, formed by O. Moeller in 1924. $40.00 pair

P 433 — Standing Devil.

P 435 I & O — Large and Small Dogs. $60.00

P 436 — Cat.

---

P 437 — Sitting Duck with a top knot.

---

P 438 — Raven.

---

P 442 — Small Arab with a Turban, shaped by Arthur Moeller in 1925. $35.00

P 440 — Penguins, seven and five holes. Scarce. $75.00

P 443 — Sitting Cat with a Bow on its neck, 1-7/8" high, produced by Arthur Moeller in 1925. $35.00

P 441 — Little Holland Man wearing a hat, accomplished by Arthur Moeller in 1925. $35.00

P 444 — Sitting Dog, 1-3/4" high, thought up by Arthur Moeller in 1925. $35.00

P447 — Elephant wearing a Crown, worked out by Arthur Moeller in 1925. Scarce. $150.00

P 445 — Small Sitting Owl, sculpted by Arthur Moeller in 1925.

P 448 — Mad Hatter.

P 446 — Tiny Chicken, designed by Arthur Moeller in 1925. Scarce. $35.00 single

P 449/1 & P 450/1— Hollander Boy (P 449/1) and Hollander Girl (P 450/1), contrived by Max Pechtold in 1925. $50.00

P 449/0 & P 450/0 — Small Hollander Boy (P 449/0) and Hollander Girl (P 450/0), 2" high. $50.00

P 449/1 & P 450/1 — These examples are shown in brown and green.

---

P 451 — Dutch Couple.

---

P 452 I & O — Happy King, by a group of sculptors in 1925.

P 453 — Woman in a High Backed Chair, built by Max Pechtold in 1925. $50.00

---

P 454 — Figure wearing a hat, 1925.

---

P 455 — Little Girl, 2" tall, created in 1925. Scarce. $50.00 single

108

P 456 — Little Sitting Boys, Salt & Pepper Shakers, sculpted in 1925. $125.00

P 457 —Little Sitting Girls holding flowers, seven and five holes for Salt & Pepper, sculpted in 1925. $125.00

P 458 — Buddha.

P 459 — Chinese Man.

P 460 — Chinese Woman.

P 462 — Young Bird.

P 463 — Chick, sculpted by Max Pechtold in 1925.

P 464 — Chick, created by Max Pechtold in 1925.

P 465 — Young Bird with Mouth Wide Open

P 466 — Young Bird with Mouth Wide Open

P 467 — Donkey?

P 468 — Stork, 3-1/2" tall Salt Shaker, carrying a Swaddled Baby Pepper Shaker.

P 469 — Girl and Dog (one piece?).

P 470 — Sitting Girl.

P 471 — Long Fish.

P 472 — Rabbit with Floppy Ears, arranged by Arthur Moeller in 1925.

P 473 — Rabbit, schemed up by Max Kohles in 1925.

P 474 — Chick, modeled by Carl Lyseck in 1925.

P 476 — Dog with big eyes.

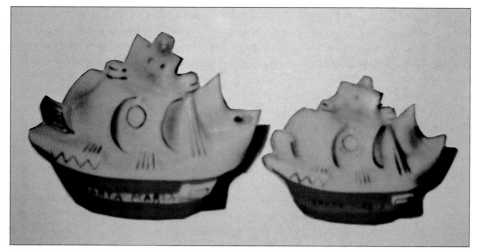

P 477 — Large Santa Maria as the Salt Shaker and a smaller one as the Pepper Shaker, carved by Max Moeller and first issued in 1925. Scarce. $200.00

P 478 — Standing Fishermen, formed by Karl Simon in 1925. $125.00

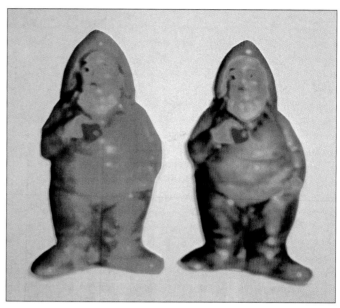

P 479 — Sitting Bulldog, planned by Arthur Moeller in 1925. $95.00

P 480 — Standing Woman wearing a hat and holding an umbrella as a cane.

P 481 — Sitting Indian smoking a pipe.

P 482 I & O — Sitting Indians, formatted by Reinhold Unger in 1925. Scarce. $65.00

P 484 I & O — Bear Cub.

P 491 — Elephant.

P 485 — Sitting Bear Cub.

P 492 — Small sitting Dachshund wearing earphones. $100.00

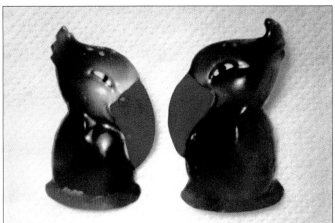

P 486 — Tropical Birds. $65.00

P 487 — Swan.

P 488 — Swan.

P 489 — Sitting Vulture.

P 493 — Sitting Boy wearing earphones. $100.00

P 490 — Sitting Duckling, modeled by
Erich Woehner in 1925. $28.00

P 494 — Sitting Girl wearing earphones. $100.00

P 498 — Large Cat with its back arched, shaped by Arthur Moeller in 1926. $39.00

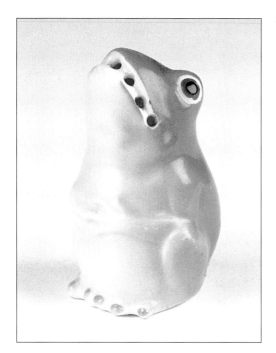

P 495 — Frog looking up, 1926. Notice the hole pattern. Scarce. $50.00 single

P 499 — Large Dog sitting, thought up by O. Moeller in 1926. $39.00

P 496 — Sitting Duck looking up, created in 1925.

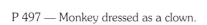

P 497 — Monkey dressed as a clown.

P 500 — Small Baby Bird waiting to be fed, hatched by Karl Simon in 1926. $29.00

P 502 — Small Crouching Dog, produced by O. Moeller in 1926. $59.00

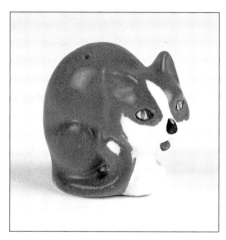

P 503 — Small Cat with its back arched, conjured up by Arthur Moeller in 1926. $65.00

P 501 — Man in Top Hat and Tails, 1926. $100.00 single.

P 504 — Parrot.

P 505 — Parrot.

P 506 — Duckling, formed by Max Pechtold in 1926.

P 509 I & O — Sitting Harlequins, with seven holes for Salt and five holes for Pepper. $50.00

P 512 — Frowning Dog.

P 513 — Smiling Dog.

P 514 — Sitting Woman in beach attire. $75.00

P 515 — Dog facing left.

P 516 — Clown, carved by Arthur Moeller in 1926.

P 517 — Clown, modeled by Arthur Moeller in 1926.

P 518 — Boy facing right.

P 511 — "Flapper" in a Blue Coat, 1926. $75.00 single.

P 519 — Boy facing left.

P 520 —Birds, flown by Karl Simon in 1926. $60.00

P 521 — Parrots.

P 522 — Bird.

P 523 — Happy Dog.

P 524 — Felix the Cat.

P 525 — Bird.

P 527 — Happy Male Cat.

P 528 — Happy Female Cat.

P 529 — Parrot.

P 530 — Bird, by Karl Simon in 1926.

P 531 — "One Piece" Salt & Pepper Shaker of a Fisherman and a Dog. Most of the "One Piece" shakers are attributed to a "combo" (combination of sculptors), because most of them are marriages of existing single shakers. This one, for instance, is made of P 478 standing Fisherman and P 381 Dog. $500.00+

P 526 — Ducks, arranged by Max Pechtold in 1926. $50.00

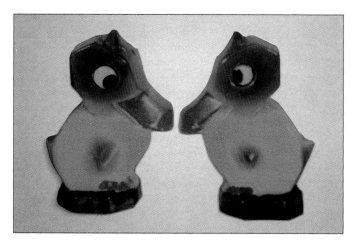

P 532 — One Piece, Two Babies in swaddling Clothes.

P 533 — One Piece, Hans and Fritz, the Katzenjammer Kids. Rare. $1,000.00 & up

P 535 — One Piece, Mother and Baby Parrots. $90.00 to $125.00

P 534 — One Piece, Duck and Duckling. $100.00

P 536 — One Piece, Mother Bird and P 500 Baby Bird. $90.00 to $125.00

P 537 — One Piece, Large Dog and Small Cat. $90.00 to $125.00

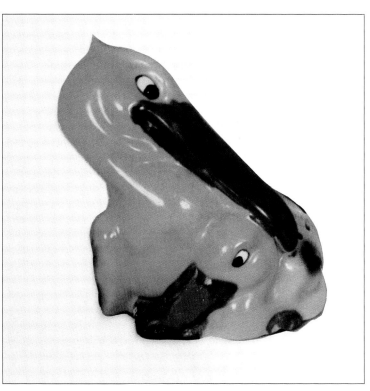

P 540 — One Piece, Mother and Baby
Pelicans. $90.00 to $125.00

P 538 — One Piece, Boy and a Soccer Ball.
Unique. $250.00

P 542 — One Piece, Boy with Earphones P 493 and
Dog with Earphones P 492. Scarce. $500.00+

P 543 — One Piece, Duck feeding a
Baby Bird. $90.00 to $125.00

---

P 544 — One Piece, Large and Small Dogs, or Bears.

---

P 546 — One Piece, Twin Cylinders.

---

P 548 — One Piece, Rabbit and an Egg.

---

P 549 — One Piece, Large Dog P 636 and Small
Dog P 637. Scarce. $150.00 to $200.00

P 547 — One Piece, Large Rabbit P 387
and Small Rabbit P 473. $80.00 to $120.00

P 550 — One Piece, Large Donkey P 640 and Small Donkey
P 641. Scarce. $150.00 to $200.00

P 551 I & O — Large and Small Bees on a base, by Moeller in 1926.

P 552 I & O — Large and Small Bees on top of Crowns, by Moeller in 1926.

P 553 I & O — Shakers with Beetles on them, by Max Moeller in 1930.

P 571 I & O — Sitting Rabbit with left ear up.

P 574 — Butler in an Apron, by Schmidt in 1930.

P 575 — Rose.

P 576 I & O — Cat in a Fur Trimmed Coat, dressed by Reinhold Unger in 1926. $65.00

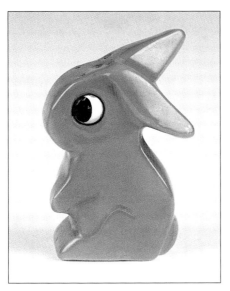

P 572 I & O — Sitting Rabbit with right ear up, by Max Paetzold in 1926. $50.00

P 573 I & O — Large Clown Heads. Rare. $145.00 to $175.00

P 577 I & O — Well Dressed Dog, created by Reinhold Unger in 1930. $65.00

P 578 I & O — Bird in a Fur Trimmed Coat, sculpted by Reinhold Unger in 1926. $65.00

P 587 — Rabbits with Base Drums, played by Max Kohles in 1926. $75.00 to $100.00

P 579 —Dutch Woman, contrived by Reinhold Unger in 1926.

P 588 — Rabbit with a Horn, directed by Max Kohles in 1926. $65.00

P 580 — 1920s Flapper Woman.

P 581 — Teddy Bear with a Banjo.

P 582 — Teddy Bear with a Banjo, facing forward.

P 583 — Teddy Bear with a Harp.

P 584 — Teddy Bear.

P 589 — Rabbit with a base Saxophone, modeled by Max Kohles in 1926.

P 585 — Teddy Bear drinking a Baby Bottle.

P 590 — Black Figure in a Top Hat.

P 586 — Teddy Bear.

P 591 — Father Christmas, by Max Moeller in 1926.

P 592 — Snowman, built by Max Moeller in 1926.

P 593 — ???, 1926.

P 595 — Knave, 1926.

P 596 — Standing Dressed Male Rabbit Salt Shaker, by Max Pechtold in 1926.

P 601 & P 602 — Sitting Elephant with trunk straight down (P601) and Sitting Elephant with trunk UP and to the LEFT (P 602), trained by Max Pechtold in 1927. (M 46 is different.) $65.00

P 603 — Bird (Stork) with a Coat on, produced by Max Pechtold in 1927.

P 604 — Bird (Stork) with a Coat on, thought up by Max Pechtold in 1927.

P 605 — Elephant, accomplished by Max Pechtold in 1927.

P 606 — Old Man.

P 607 — Old Man.

P 617 — Butterfly.

P 618 — Butterfly.

P 619 — Snarling Cat, riled up by Arthur Moeller in 1927.

P 620 — Grinning Cat, petted by Arthur Moeller in 1927.

P 597 — Standing Dressed Girl Rabbit Pepper Shaker, created by Max Pechtold in 1926. Rare. $100.00 single.

P 598 — Duckling, planned by Max Pechtold in 1927

P 599 — Buzzard.

P 600 — Buzzard.

P 621 — Woman with Hands on her Hips.

P 622 — Arab Girl with Flowers in her Hands, shaped by Max Moeller in 1927. $65.00

P 624 I & O — Musicians playing Base Drums, seven-hole Salt and five-hole Pepper Shakers AND Place Card Holders. Rare. $200.00 per pair.

P 623 I & O — Bellhop with Flowers in his left hand, carved by Max Moeller in 1927. These come in three colors, all as Salt & Pepper, with seven and five holes. $35.00 each

P 625 I & O — Musicians playing Base Saxophones, seven-hole Salt and five-hole Pepper Shakers AND Place Card Holders. Rare. $200.00 per pair.

P 626 I & O — Musicians playing Alto Saxophones, seven-hole Salt and five-hole Pepper Shakers AND Place Card Holders. Rare. $200.00 per pair.

P 627 — By a combo, in 1927.

P 628 I & O — Dressed Chickens, by a combo in 1927. Rare. $75.00 to $100.00 single.

P 629 & P 630— Kneeling Elf holding on to a toadstool with head turned to the right as a Salt Shaker with seven holes (P629) and Kneeling Elf holding on to a toadstool with head turned to the left, as a Pepper Shaker with five holes (P 630). Rare. $150.00

P 632 — Lady with a Purse and a Cane, by a combo in 1928.

P 633 — Penguin.

P 634 — Large Sitting Cow. $50.00

P 635 — Small Sitting Calf. $50.00

P 639 — Sitting Dog. $45.00

P 636 & P 637— Large Sitting Dog (P 636) and Small Sitting Dog (P 637), raised by Moeller in 1927. $80.00 pair.

P 638 — Sitting Dog.

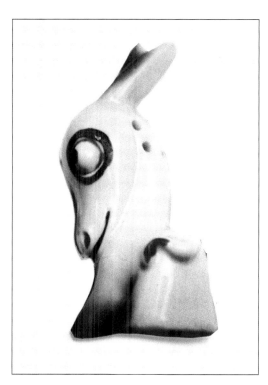

P 640 — Large sitting Donkey. $50.00

P 641 — Small sitting Donkey. $50.00

P 656 I & O — Chinese Urns, spun by Lofl in 1928. $45.00

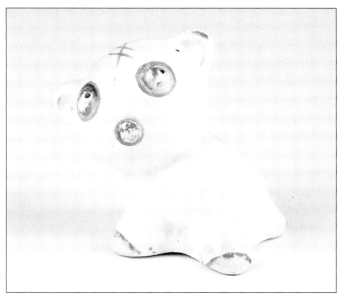

P 642 — Koala Bear. Scarce. $100.00

P 657 I & O — Chinese Urns, thrown by Lofl in 1928. $45.00

P 643 — Panda Bear.

P 658 I & O — Chinese Urns, turned by Lofl in 1928.

P 644 — Penguin.

P 662 — Ribbed Shakers.

P 651 — Black Forest Girl.

P 668 — Egg Shaped Shaker with horizontal stripes.

P 669 — Cylindrical Shaker, made about 1929.

P 670 A & B — Large and Small Cactus, pricked by Erich Hofmann in 1929. $40.00

P 671 — Bull Dog, by Erich Hofmann in 1929

P 672 — Egg on a Base.

P 673 — Girl's Head.

P 674 — Bull Dog.

P 675 — Bull Dog.

P 676 A & B — Cactus Salt & Pepper Shakers, dried out by Schmidt in 1930. $40.00

P 677 — Cactus five-hole Pepper Shaker, by Schmidt in 1930.

P 678 — Cactus seven-hole Salt Shaker, by Schmidt in 1930.

P 679 I & O — Boy in a Derby Hat.

P 680 — Bird, by Karl Simon in 1930.

P 681 — Sitting Dog on a Base that says "I'm in Love," by Moeller in 1930.

P 682 — Sitting Dog on a Base with a "saying" on it, by Moeller in 1930.

P 683 — Sitting Dog on a Base with a "saying" on it, by Moeller in 1930.

P 684 — Sitting Dog on a Base with a "saying" on it, by Moeller in 1930.

P 685 — Bird, by L. ?, in 1930.

P 686 — (duplicate number) Arab.

P 686 I & O — (duplicate number) Birds , by L. ?, in 1930.

P 687 — Bird, by L. ?, 1930.

P 688 — Bird, by Karl Simon in 1930.

P 689 — Squirrel, by Barth in 1930.

P 690 — Gandhi, by a combo in 1930.

P 691 I & O — Mickey Mouse, by a combo, in 1930.

P 695 & P 696 — Adamson (1920s cartoon character, also known as "Silent Sam"), with hat on as the Salt Shaker, and with hat off as the Pepper Shaker, by a combo in 1931. $65.00

P 692 — Mickey Mouse, by Bauer in 1930. Rare. $150.00+

P 693 — Rabbit, by a combo in 1930.

P 694 — Chick.

P 697/0 (& P 704/0) — Soldier with a Rifle on his shoulder as the Salt Shaker, and P 704 Soldier with a Drum as the Pepper Shaker, by Arthur Moeller in 1931. $55.00

P 702 I & O — Large and Small Man Playing a French Horn as Salt & Pepper, by A. Moeller in 1931.

P 697/1 — Same figures, in a larger size. $60.00

P 703 A & B — Maggie and Jiggs, comic strip characters by George McManus. (I & O indicates that they were made in two sizes.) B = Maggie as the Pepper Shaker, while A = Jiggs as the Salt Shaker, sculpted in 1931. $100.00 each

P 698 I & O — Large Fish as a Salt Shaker and small one as the Pepper Shaker, by Arthur Moeller in 1931. These come in many different colors. $30.00

P 704 — Soldier, see P 697.

P 699 — Jockey in riding clothes, by Arthur Moeller in 1931.

P 705 I & O — Penguins, by a combo in 1931.

P 700 — Snail, slowly made by Bauer in 1931.

P 706 — Raven, by Barth in 1930.

P 701 I & O — Large and Small Man Playing a Base Fiddle as Salt & Pepper, by A. Moeller in 1931.

P 707 — Barrel, coopered by Karl Simon in 1931.

P 708 — Old Farmer, by Reinhold Unger in 1931.

P 709 — Old Farmer's Wife, by Reinhold Unger in 1931.

P 710 — Sparrow, by a combo in 1931.

P 711 I & O — Charlie Chaplin as Salt & Pepper Shakers, molded by Moeller in 1932.

P 712 — Sailor, piped aboard by Moeller in 1932.

P 713 — Sitting Rabbit, by Reinhold Unger in 1932.

P 714/0 — Chef with a Spoon as Salt Shaker and P 731/0 Cook with an Apron as Pepper Shaker, by a combo in 1932. $40.00

P 714/1 & P 731/1 — Same figures in a larger size. $45.00

P 715 — Rabbit, by a combo in 1932.

P 716 — Pig, by a combo in 1932.

P 717 — Scottish Terrier Pessimist, by Moeller in 1932.

P 718 — Scottish Terrier Optimist, by Moeller in 1932.

P 719 — Chicken, by Reinhold Unger in 1931.

P 720 — Dog, by Reinhold Unger in 1931.

P 721 — Chicken, by Moeller in 1932.

P 722 — Jockey, by Moeller in 1932.

P 723 — Scottish Terrier, by Karl Simon in 1932.

P 724 —see M 412

P 725 — Sitting Dog.

P 726 — Walking Figure with a "Crown of Flowers," decorated by Moeller in 1931.

P 727 — Duck, by a combo in 1932.

P 728 — Rabbit, by a combo in 1932.

P 729 — Rabbit, by a combo in 1932.

P 730 — Rabbit, by Moeller in 1932.

P 731 — Girl Cook, sautéed by Reinhold Unger in 1933.

P 732 — Begging Dog with flowers in his paws, by Moeller in 1933.

P 733 — Standing Drummer, by Karl Simon in 1933.

P 734 — Standing Man, by Karl Simon in 1933.

P 735 — Rabbit, by a combo in 1933.

P 736 — Kid in a Bathing suit, by a combo in 1933.

P 737 — Cat with its back up, by Moeller in 1933.

P 738 — Dog up on his haunches, by a combo in 1933.

P 739 — Tropical Fish, by Reinhold Unger in 1933.

P 740 — Raven, by Moeller, the "New Model" was created in 1933.

P 741 — Smooth "Pear shaped" Jar Shaker, shaped by Moeller in 1933.

P 742 — Cylindrical Jar with three rings around it, by Reinhold Unger in 1933.

P 743 — Pig as a Shaker, modeled in 1933.

P 744 — sitting Pig, slopped by Moeller in 1933.

P 745 — Rabbit with a Parasol, by a combo in 1933.

P 746 — Tyrolean Man, by Moeller in 1933.

P 747 — Rabbit with ears straight up, by Moeller in 1933,

P 748 — Chalice, by Moeller in 1933,

P 749 — Moor (black man with his hands on his stomach), modeled by Moeller in 1933.

P 750 — Bride and Groom, by a combo in 1933.

P 751 — Cat Head tilted to the right, by Reinhold Unger in 1933.

P 752 — Cat Head tilted to the left, by Reinhold Unger in 1933.

P 753 — Sitting Cat, by a combo in 1933.

P 754 — Dog on a Kettle Drum with a Flower Pot, by a combo in 1933.

TRI 6 A B C D —
Snowman and Snow-
woman on a Clover
Shaped Tray, with a
Snowball shaped
Mustard Pot. The TRI
prefix is used as the
artist who designed the
subjects was Walter Trier.
The sculptors were
Naumann and Horst
Ashermann, in 1956.
$500.00+

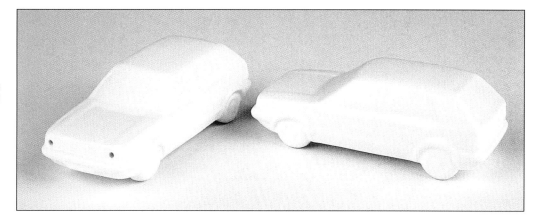

Volkswagen in a glazed white, as
Salt & Pepper Shakers. $50.00

WELL 302 A B C — Bottles of Wine
Shakers and a Basket of Grapes Mustard
Pot, by Adolf Kuehn in 1953, based on
the design of Hanns Welling.

131

# Numerical Order

The "number" prefix was created in the early 1970s to supercede the letter prefix.

70 is one of the prefixes used to designate three pieces that include Salt & Pepper Shakers, when they are on a tray or in a basket. Only a few 70 numbers were issued, as they were soon superceded by the 77 Prefix.

70 250 — New version of M 250.

70 263 — Same as 77 550.

70 264 — Same as 77 549

70 042 — Newer version of M 42 A B C D. $40.00 to 55.00

70 446 — GRA 109 A & B, Salt & Pepper shakers in the Plastic Basket for two pieces.

The Prefix 71 designates Egg Cups, and also two shakers on a tray or in a basket. It was soon superceded by the 78 Prefix.

70 045 — New version of L Mun 45 $125.00

71 001 — Rabbit with Ceramic Basket, holding two shakers. $20.00 to $25.00

71 002 — Rabbit with an Egg Cup Base
and a Salt Shaker Top. $30.00 to $40.00

71 015 — Newly sculptured P 179 White and Black Cats (without
whiskers) on T 71/1 Tray. $18.00 to $22.00

71 003 — Brown Rabbit Shaker sitting on a ceramic Basket Base
which is an Egg Cup. $25.00 to $35.00

71 003 — White Rabbit Shaker sitting on a ceramic Basket Base
which is an Egg Cup.

71 117 01 — New version of M 117 Pink
Pigs on T 71/1 Tray. $18.00

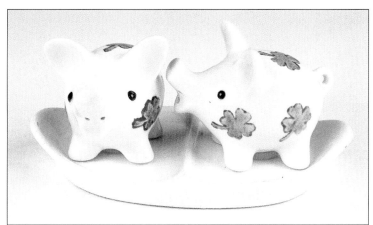

71 117 02 — White Pigs with Clovers on
them, on T 71/1 Tray. $18.00

71 117 08 — White Pigs with Flowers on them, on T 71/1 Tray.

71 119 — New version of M 119.

71 120 — New version of M 120.

71 202 — P 90 B & C in the small Plastic Oval Basket. $18.00

71 200 — Chimney Sweeps in the medium Oval Plastic Basket. $28.00 to $35.00

71 203 — Stylized Ducks in the small Oval Plastic Basket. $28.00 to $30.00

71 201 — Pink Pigs in the small Oval Plastic Basket. $20.00

71 204 01 — same as DIS 204.

---

71 204 02 — Same mold Rabbits in green and purple.

---

71 215 — P 179 Cats in the small Oval Plastic Basket. $35.00

71 217 — P 184 Kittens in the small Oval Plastic Basket. $22.00

71 216 — P 150 Carp in the medium Plastic Oval Basket. $20.00

71 226 — M 36 A & B in the small Oval Plastic Basket. $18.00

71 235 — P 151 in the medium Plastic Oval Basket. $20.00

---

71 251 — same as M 251 A B C.

---

71 265 — Friar Tuck in the small Oval Plastic Basket. $18.00

71 278 — Roosters in the medium Plastic Oval Basket. $25.00 to $30.00

73 is the Prefix assigned to PAIRS of Salt & Pepper Shakers.

---

73 005 — Cups as Salt & Pepper Shakers.

---

73 017 & 73 020 — Swimming Ducks, Salt & Pepper Shakers.

---

73 018 & 019 (re-issued P 18 & 19) — Boy and Girl in traditional dress, Salt & Pepper Shakers. $15.00

73 020 — See 73 017.

73 022 A & B (re-issued L Mun 22) —
Munich Monks Salt & Pepper. $22.00

73 024 & 025 — Brown Owls, by Helmut Fischer in 1983. $25.00

73 024 & 025 — White Owls from the same mold. $25.00

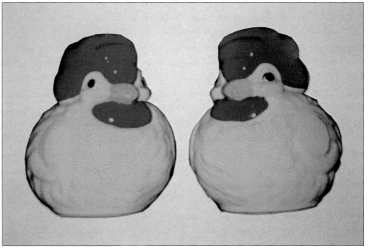

73 027 & 028 — Chickens, by Jochen
Bauer in 1984. $30.00 to $40.00

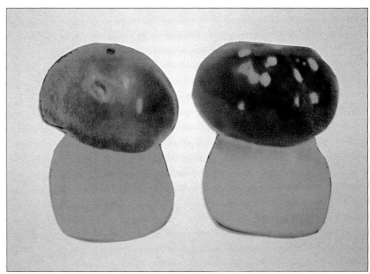

73 029 & 030 — Mushrooms, by K. Sauer
in 1985. $15.00 to $20.00

73 031 and 73 032 — Mickey and Minnie as shakers.

73 034 & 035 — Baguette Boy and Girl as Salt & Pepper, by J. Gotze in 1984. $35.00 to $40.00

73 043 & 73 044 — Re-sculpted P 93, by G. Siefert in 1986. $60.00

73 040 — Re-sculpted DIS 40.

73 045 & 046 — ALOISIUS.

73 041 & 042 — Re-sculpted P 86, by G. Siefert in 1986. $70.00

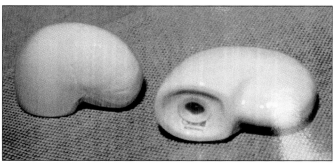

73 047 & 048 — Mussel or Conch Shells as Salt & Pepper Shakers. $22.00

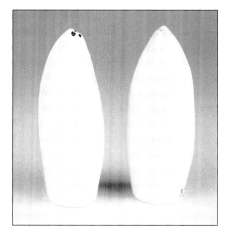

73 049 & 050 — Brussels Chicory Salt & Pepper Shakers, by R. & L. Misic in 1988. $15.00 to $20.00

73 088 & 089 — Re-sculpted P 189, by
Gerhard Wittmann in 1983. $75.00

73 182 & 183 — Re-sculpted P 183, by
Gerhard Wittmann in 1982. $20.00

73 184 — Ref. P 184 Kittens. $25.00

73 090 — Same as M 90 B & C.

73 095 & 096 — Refer to P 95 A & B.

73 097 — Refer to P 97 A & B.

73 116 A & B — Small Pigs (Ref. P 743) with flowers decorating
the sides, by G. Skrobek in 1984.

73 150 A & B — Large and Small Carp Salt & Pepper Shakers.
(Re-sculpted P 150) $15.00

73 153 A & B — Same as P 153 A & B. $20.00

73 195 A & B — Roosters (striped). $28.00 to 35.00

73 195 A & B — Roosters (solid color). $25.00 to $35.00

73 231 — Re-issued E 231, Chick as a shaker. $15.00

73 248 & 249 — Fisherman and Woman, by H. P. Winkenbach in 1983. $24.00 to $34.00

73 250 & 251 — Chef as a Salt Shaker and Female Cook as the Pepper Shaker, by H. P. Winkenbach in 1983. $35.00

73 232 A & B — Chimney Sweep Salt & Pepper Shakers. $20.00 to $25.00

73 242 & 243 — Butler and Chambermaid, by H. P. Winkenbach in 1983. $25.00 to $35.00

73 252 & 253 — Boy with Derby and Girl with Hat as Salt & Pepper Shakers, by Helmut Fischer in 1983. $18.00 to $28.00

73 400 & 401 — Wine Barrels decorated with Grapes, three-hole Salt and two-hole Pepper Shakers. $25.00 to $35.00

73 514 — Cylindrical shaped "Burgund" Salt & Pepper Shakers. $15.00 for the plain olive drab color, up to 45.00 for the nicely decorated pair shown.

73 514 — Shakers in a "Basket for Two."

The 77 Prefix was assigned to four or more piece sets, including trays and baskets.

77 232 — FLORAL three pieces of GRA 109 with the POINSET-TIA pattern, on T 90 Tray. $40.00

77 233 — Three pieces of GRA 109 with the BOUNTIFUL pattern, on T 90 Tray. $40.00

77 235 — GRA 109 A B C in the TYROL pattern, on T 90 Tray. $40.00

77 236 — GRA 109 A B C in the
SPANIEN pattern, on T 90 Tray. $40.00

77 501 (M 206) — M 86 A B C in the long Woven Wicker Basket.
$50.00

77 505 (M 210) — M 93 A B C in the long Woven Wicker Basket.
$50.00

77 530 (M/GRA 432) — Salt & Pepper Shakers and Mustard Pot
with the BOUNTIFUL pattern, in the Triangle Woven Wicker
Basket. $60.00 to $80.00

77 517 — Six pieces in a basket

77 533 FLORAL (M/GRA 431) — Three pieces of GRA 109 with
the POINSETTIA pattern in the long Metal Basket. The basket is
rare. $65.00 to $90.00

77 534 (M/GRA 431) — Three pieces of GRA 109 with the
BOUNTIFUL pattern in the long Metal Basket. Rare basket.
$65.00 to $90.00

77 520 (M 428) — M 114 A B C in the RARE long Metal Basket.
$65.00 to $100.00

77 528 (M 237) — M 107 A B C in the Woven Wicker Triangle
Basket. Basket is scarce. $90.00

77 537 — GRA 109 A B C with the SPANIEN
pattern, in the Triangle Plastic Basket. $40.00

77 542 (M 250) — P 200 Shakers with matching Condiment Pot in the Triangle Plastic Basket. $40.00 to $50.00

77 544 — GRA 109 A B C in the long Metal Basket. $60.00 to $80.00

77 543 (M/GRA 260) — GRA 147 A & B and GRA 148 Mustard Pot in the Triangle Plastic Basket. $35.00 to $50.00

77 547 — GRA 109 A B C Salt & Pepper Shakers, along with the Mustard Pot, with the TYROL pattern in the Triangle Plastic Basket. $40.00 to $60.00

143

77 548 — GRA 109 A B C Salt & Pepper Shakers, along with the Mustard Pot, with the TYROL pattern in the long Metal Basket. $60.00 to $90.00

77 549 (Also shown as number 70 263 ) — Pink colored Pigs, Salt & Pepper Shakers and Condiment Pot, in the Triangle Plastic Basket. $35.00 to $50.00

77 550 (Also shown as number 70 264 ) — Pigs with Clovers on the sides, Salt & Pepper Shakers and Mustard Pot, in the Triangle Plastic Basket. $40.00 to $55.00

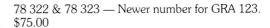

77 553 — GRA 179 A & B, along with the matching Condiment Pot, in the Triangle Plastic Basket. $40.00

77 555 — GRA 179 A & B, along with the matching Condiment Pot, in the long Metal Basket. $65.00

These three pieces in the Woven Triangle Wicker Basket have no number incised. They are marked Merkebach Salzglasur, Goebel, W. Germany.

78 is the Prefix generally used for three piece sets.

78 320 & 78 321 — Newer number for GRA 125. $75.00

78 322 & 78 323 — Newer number for GRA 123. $75.00

78 372 & 373 — Small white pigs decorated with clovers, by Gerhard Skrobek.

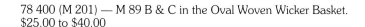

78 400 (M 201) — M 89 B & C in the Oval Woven Wicker Basket. $25.00 to $40.00

78 401 (M 202) — M 90 B & C Chick and Rabbit Salt & Pepper Shakers in the Oval Woven Wicker Basket. $25.00 to $40.00

78 402 (M 203) — Stylized Duck Salt & Pepper Shakers in the Oval Woven Wicker Basket. $30.00 to $45.00

78 403 (M 212) — P 420/0 and P 420/2/0 in the Oval Woven Wicker Basket. $20.00 to 40.00

78 405 (M 214) — M 86 B & C in the Oval Woven Wicker Basket. $20.00 to $40.00

78 406 (M 215) — P 179 White Cat with whiskers Salt Shaker and Black Cat with whiskers Pepper Shaker, in the Oval Woven Wicker Basket. $25.00 to $45.00

78 407 (M 216) — P 150 A & B Carp Salt & 'Pepper Shakers in the Oval Woven Wicker Basket. $20.00

78 408 (M 217) — P 184 A & B Kitten Salt & Pepper Shakers in the Oval Woven Wicker Basket. $28.00

78 411 (M 226) — Squirrel Salt Shaker and Pine Cone Pepper Shaker in the Oval Woven Wicker Basket. $35.00

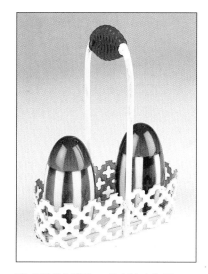

78 415 (M 429) — P 191 A & B in the Oval Metal Basket. Basket is rare. $50.00

78 422 (M 235) — White and Black Poodle Salt & Pepper Shakers in the Oval Woven Wicker Basket. $18.00 to $22.00

78 424 (M 236) — M 107 B & C in the Oval Woven Wicker Basket. $35.00 to $45.00

78 425 (M 238) — P 196 A & B Standing Pigs in the Oval Woven Wicker Basket. $35.00 to $50.00

78 427 (M/GRA 232) — GRA 109 Salt & Pepper Shakers with the BOUNTIFUL pattern, in the Oval Woven Wicker Basket. $25.00 to $40.00

78 429 (DIS 40 or M 204) — Red and Yellow Rabbits (Thumper) in the Oval Woven Wicker Basket. $45.00

78 431 (M/GRA 432) — GRA 109 FLORAL Salt & Pepper, with the Poinsettia pattern, in the Oval Metal Basket. $50.00

78 432 (M/GRA 432) — GRA 109 Salt & Pepper, with the BOUNTIFUL pattern, in the rare Oval Metal Basket. $50.00

78 433 (M/GRA 243) — GRA 125 Rabbits in the Oval Woven Wicker Basket. $50.00 to $65.00

78 434 (M/GRA 244) — GRA 123 Fox, in the Oval Woven Wicker Basket. $50.00 to $65.00

78 436 (M/GRA 247) — GRA 127 A & B Salt & Pepper Shakers in
the Oval Woven Wicker Basket. $55.00 to $75.00

78 438 (M/GRA 249) — GRA 129 A & B Salt & Pepper Shakers in
the Oval Woven Wicker Basket. $55.00 to $75.00

78 437 (M/GRA 248) — GRA 128 A & B Salt & Pepper Shakers in
the Oval Woven Wicker Basket. $55.00 to $75.00

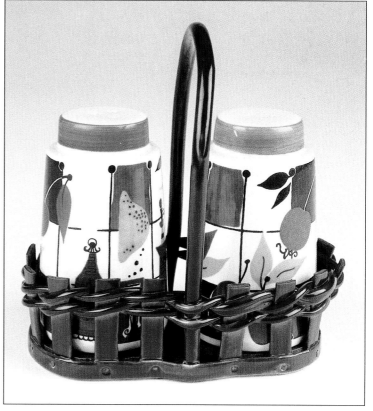

78 440 — GRA 109 A & B Salt & Pepper Shakers in
the medium Oval Plastic Basket. $22.00 to $38.00

147

78 441 (M 251) — P 200 A & B Salt & Pepper
Shakers in the medium Oval Plastic Basket.
$22.00 to $35.00

78 444 (M/GRA 261) — GRA 147 A & B in the medium Oval
Plastic Basket. $25.00 to $35.00

78 445 — GRA 109 with the SPANIEN
pattern in the Oval Metal Basket. $50.00

78 446 — GRA 109 A & B Salt & Pepper Shakers with the
TYROL pattern, in the medium Oval Plastic Basket. $25.00 35.00

78 447 — GRA 109 A & B Salt &
Pepper Shakers with the TYROL
pattern, in the RARE Oval Metal Basket.
$55.00 to $75.00

78 450 — GRA 179 A & B Salt & Pepper Shakers, in the Oval Plastic Basket. $20.00 to $35.00

78 452 — GRA 179 A & B Salt & Pepper Shakers, in the Oval Metal Basket. $50.00

78 459 — Same as M 265 A B C. $25.00

78 650 — Newer number for 71 117 01, Pink Pigs Salt & Pepper, standing on Tray T 71/1.
$20.00

78 658 — Newer number for 71 117 02, Pigs with Clovers on them, standing on Tray T 71/1. $20.00

78 700 — GRA 109 A, three-hole salt shaker, & B, two-hole pepper shaker, decorated in the "Tyrol" pattern.

78 724 & 78 725 — Same as P 191 A & B. $20.00

78 731 & 78 732 — GRA 109 "Bountiful." $18.00

78 735 & 78 736 — GRA 109 "Floral." $18.00

78 755 & 78 756 — GRA 109 "Spanien." $18.00

78 767 & 78 768 — Same as GRA 147 A & B. $20.00

041 807 — Functional Salt & Pepper Shakers. $20.00

## Friars

For ease of reference and comparison, all of the Friar Tuck shakers are grouped together in this section.

M 42 A B C D — First issued in 1954 with Friars that wore sandals exposing their toes, designed by Reinhold Unger. This early version has the RARE Ceramic Spoon. $75.00 to $125.00 w/toes AND SPOON.

M 42 A B C D — Set was soon redesigned in 1955 to eliminate the toes, and the extra painting required. The Mustard Pot still split at the shoulders. $55.00

70 042 — Newer version of M 42 A B C D. The Mustard Pot splits at the neck. $40.00 to 55.00

M 119 B C D — Variation in blue. $35.00 to $40.00

M 42 A B C D — Produced as Cardinal Tuck from 1960-1965. These are much scarcer than the Friars, and are worth more. $200.00 to $350.00

M 265 A B C — Consists of the P 153 I & O Friars in the small Oval Woven Basket. $23.00

M 119 B C D — Consists of P 153/l Large & P 153/O Small Friar on T 71/1 Tray. $25.00 to $30.00

P 153/0 — Friar Tuck, same size, three and two holes. First created by Reinhold Unger in 1954, with sandals on and toes exposed. By 1955, the toes disappeared. Scarce with toes exposed. $35.00

P 153 I & O — Large and Small Friars
with toes exposed, 1954. $35.00

P 153 A & B — Cardinal Tuck, released in 1960 in Europe, then
released in the US in 1963, but discontinued in 1965. Scarce.
$125.00 to $150.00

P 153/0 — Friars, same size with toes exposed,
in white glazed finish. Scarce. $45.00

P 176 A & B — Friar Tuck carrying Books,
by Theo Menzenbach in 1957. $45.00

P 153 A & B — Changed in 1955 to "Black Shoes."
They were issued in this version, and also two the same
size. These versions were produced until 1989 so the
supply is "plentiful." $15.00 to $25.00

P 176 A & B — Cardinal Tuck carrying Books. $125.00

## Silver Clad

There are no records at Goebel to indicate that they created the Silver Clad Salt & Pepper Sets. At this time, it is not known what company created the sets. The silver on the Goebel sets is not just painted on; it has about .005" (1/10 mm) thickness and can be "felt" with your fingernail. Some of the silver clad pieces have "STERLING" stamped into the silver, in tiny letters. We have observed that each silver clad shaker is smaller than the un-clad piece of the SAME number.

P 189 A & B — Friar Tuck. The one playing the flute is the Salt Shaker. $90.00

73 088 & 089 — Re-sculpted P 189, by Gerhard Wittmann in 1983. $75.00

M 6 A B C D — Holland Condiment Set, consists of an octagonal "Windmill" Mustard Pot and a Dutch Boy and Girl Salt & Pepper by Arthur Moeller, on Max Pechtold's 1927 Tray. $500.00+

71 265 — Friar Tuck in the small Oval Plastic Basket. $18.00

Silver P 18 & 19 — Tyrolean Boy and Girl, by Erich Lautensack in 1936. $40.00 to $50.00

Silver P 36 A & B — Norwegian Boy and Girl, by Reinhold Unger in 1936. $55.00 to $75.00

Silver P 97 A & B — Hugging Tyrolean Boy and Girl, by Reinhold Unger in 1950. (This Boy is not clad.) $75.00 pair

Silver P 37 A & B — Dutch Boy and Girl, by Erich Lautensack in 1937. The pair on the left has the pre-war hole pattern of seven for Salt and five for Pepper, while the right hand pair has the post-war hole pattern of three and two. $50.00 to $60.00

Silver P 109 A & B — Bashful Tyrolean Boy and Girl, by Arthur Moeller in 1950. $70.00 to $90.00

Silver P 90 A & B — White and Black Dogs with silver clad feet, by Arthur Moeller in 1950. $60.00 to $70.00

Silver P 96 A & B — Boy and Girl Skiers, by Arthur Moeller in 1950. $70.00 to $85.00

Silver P 123 A & B — Boy and Girl with Grapes, by Karl Wagner in 1951. $70.00 to $90.00

Silver P 137 A — Sitting Frog, by Karl Wagner in 1952. $50.00

Silver P 134 A & B — Three examples of cladding on these pairs, made by Karl Wagner in 1952. $45.00 to $65.00

Silver P 135 A & B — Mountain Climber Boy and Girl, by Karl Wagner in 1952. $65.00 to $85.00

Silver P 138 A & B — Black Forest Boy and Girl, by Hans Zetzmann in 1952. $70.00 to $90.00

Silver P 169 A & B — Swedish Boy and Girl, by Karl Wagner in 1956. $100.00 to $110.00

Silver P 414 I & O — Large and Small Pelicans, by O. Moeller in 1924. $75.00 to $80.00

Silver P 387 A — Sitting Rabbit, by Max Moeller in 1924. $70.00

Silver P 435 I & O — Small and Large Dogs, by O. Moeller in 1924. $75.00 to $90.00.

Silver P 411 A & B — Young Ducks, by Erich Wohner in 1924. $50.00 to $60.00

Silver P 449/1 & P 450/1 — Dutch Boy and Girl, by Max Pechtold in 1925. $75.00

Silver P 449/0 & P 450/0 —
Dutch Boy and Girl, by Max
Pechtold in 1925. $75.00.

Silver P 636 & P 637 — Large and Small Dogs, by
Arthur Moeller in 1927. $70.00 to $80.00

Silver P 698 — Three variations of Clad Fish, by Arthur Moeller in 1931. $50.00 pair

# Trays

Many sets have trays that are unique to that set, or that are actually part of the Mustard Pot. These can be seen where there is a picture of that set.

The basic molds for the eleven trays shown here were used for many different sets. These may help to identify a correct tray.

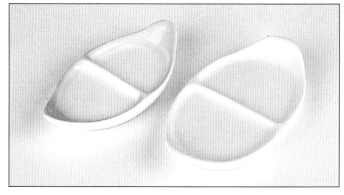

Left: T 71/0 (4-1/4" wide), same mold used for M 50 C
Right: T 71/1 (4-1/2" wide), same mold used for M 60 D, M 63 D, and M 117

Left: M 59 D (4-3/8" wide), same mold used for Bull 323, Kau 11, and M 65
Center: M 42 D (5-1/2" wide), same mold used for M 111, M 115, and T 94/1
Right: M 46 D (4-1/2" wide), same mold used for M 2, M 6/0, M 26, and M 78

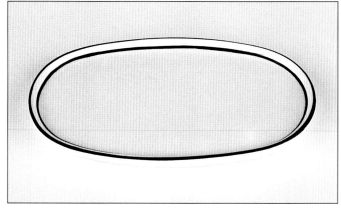

M 43 C (6-3/4" wide), same mold used for T 69.

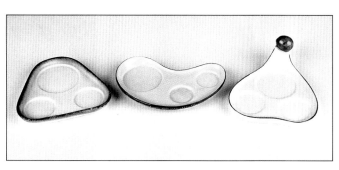

Left: M 22 D (4-1/2" wide), same mold used for M 20 D and M 24 D
Center: Hol 73 D (5-1/2" wide), same mold used for M 65 D
Right: M 86 D (4-1/2" wide), same mold used for M 52, M 62, M 72, and M 92 W

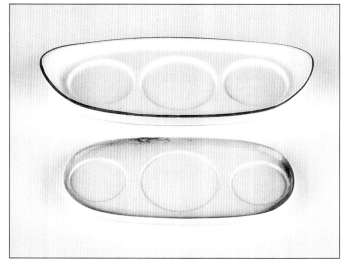

Top: T 90 (8" wide), same mold used for 77 236
Bottom: M 56 D (6-1/4" wide), same mold used for M 48 D and M 64 D

158

# Baskets

The pre-war sets and some early post-war sets were issued in Woven Wicker Baskets.

Shown here are three sizes of the Oval Woven Wicker Baskets: the Small Oval, Medium Oval, and Long for three pieces.

Around 1950, the baskets were changed to plastic with wooden bottoms. Shown here are a small White, a Small Dark, and a Medium White.

On the left is the Plastic Triangle Basket and on the right is the Woven Wicker Triangle Basket.

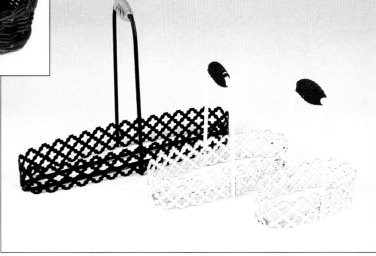

The rare Metal Baskets, for five pieces, three pieces, and two pieces.

# In Memory

The authors, Hubert center and Clara on the right, with "Mom"
McHugh, at the Salt & Pepper Collectors Convention in July 2004.

In Memory, Eva J. McHugh, March 1912 – November 2004